# WRITE A SELF-HELP BOOK IN 14 DAYS!

## by Lisa Daily

Copyright © 2024 by Lisa Daily, Quinn Daily, Elle Daily. All rights reserved.

No portion of this book may be reproduced in any form without written permission from the publisher or author, except as permitted by U.S. copyright law.

This publication is designed to provide accurate and authoritative information in regard to the subject matter covered. It is sold with the understanding that neither the author nor the publisher is engaged in rendering legal, investment, accounting or other professional services. While the publisher and author have used their best efforts in preparing this book, they make no representations or warranties with respect to the accuracy or completeness of the contents of this book and specifically disclaim any implied warranties of merchantability or fitness for a particular purpose. No warranty may be created or extended by sales representatives or written sales materials. The advice and strategies contained herein may not be suitable for your situation. You should consult with a professional when appropriate. Neither the publisher nor the author shall be liable for any loss of profit or any other commercial damages, including but not limited to special, incidental, consequential, personal, or other damages.

Library of Congress Cataloging-in-Publication Data has been applied for this ISBN, 979-8-9886398

For international rights and translations inquiries, contact:

rights@lisadailybooks.com

**To you,**
**for sharing your wisdom, chasing your dreams, and daring to make someone else's life better.**

# Contents

1. You Can Write a Best-Selling Self-Help Book — 1
2. The Struggle is Real. But Not Inevitable. — 12
3. Your Secret Weapon! The Creative Work Plan — 20
4. Brainstorming Your Catchy, Benefit-Driven Title & Action Plan Name — 47
5. Bestseller Academy Blueprint — 77
6. Before You Start Writing, Contemplate Reader Magnets — 88
7. How to Write Your First Chapters — 98
8. The Meat! Your Action Plan for the Reader — 117
9. Anatomy of an Action Plan Chapter — 126
10. Your Final Chapters — 142
11. Create Your Reader Magnets — 151
12. Create Your Workbook — 160
13. Decide whether to publish yourself or traditionally — 171

| | | |
|---|---|---|
| 14. | The Parking Lot (aka, FAQ) | 183 |
| 15. | Resources to Help You Write Your Self-Help Book & Build Your Business | 193 |

# Chapter 1

# You Can Write a Best-Selling Self-Help Book

The email arrived late on a Sunday night:

*"This is a shoot-for-the-moon request, but I have to write a non-fiction book in 11 days in order to have it ready in time for a workshop I'm giving in late September.*

*I've been struggling with adapting the workshop/speech into a workable non-fiction book and your <u>self-help book video</u> was a BREAKTHROUGH moment in the outlining process for me.*

*Could you tell me more about your coaching process and whether you'd be available to help me meet this gnarly deadline?"*

*—Theodora*

I will confess I love a good challenge, so *of course* I said yes.

The author who had sent the email was a big, bestselling romance author who had hit the *USA Today* list multiple times, had legions of adoring fans, and was earning high six figures from her books.

But despite the fact that she was already a professional author with dozens of novels to her name, she was struggling with how to structure and write her self-help book -- and was up against a deadline that was bearing down quickly.

**Maybe you can relate. You've got a great idea, but no idea how to turn it into a book. You need it done yesterday. I totally get it.**

Theodora and I worked diligently for the 11 days, and by the end, she had written an incredible book called *7-Figure Fiction*, which:

- became a bestseller,

- was the talk of the conference where she spoke (Novelists Inc),

- and within the space of a year had become part of the vernacular for fiction writers everywhere.

If you've been to a writing conference in the last few years and heard one of the speakers mention "Universal Fantasy" or "butter", you're seeing firsthand the impact of Theodora Taylor's incredible book, *7-Figure Fiction*.

What's more, she turned that one little book into a mini-empire that now includes paid speaking engagements, a course, a workbook, a paid Substack, and multiple other genre-specific books for romance, sci-fi, etc.

An *entire business* built on just *one* self-help book.

(See it for yourself right here: 7FigureFiction.com)

Can you imagine all the incredible possibilities for your business? Me too.

## Imagine this

What if you could **attract your ideal clients** and buyers 24/7 with little effort, **become the go-to expert in your niche** or topic, and **open dozens of new revenue streams**?

• **What if you could skip right to the important stuff** (like a VIP pass!) as you write your book and save yourself countless hours? Know exactly how to structure your self-help book, what you need to include, the secret to writing a life-changing book, and what mistakes to avoid so you can write your book in just two quick weeks (not months or years.)

• **What if you could warm up thousands of potential clients at a time**, while you sleep or go on vacation? No more wasted looky-loo sales calls sucking up your day. Your book is the very best introduction potential clients will ever get to you — and the leads it generates will already be primed and eager to buy your higher-priced offerings.

• **What if you could easily create new revenue streams?** You can create dozens of new products by repurposing the ideas in your book, including workbooks, courses, products, mastermind groups, coaching packages, apps, and more.

## Writing my first self-help book changed my life

My very first self-help book was a dating advice book that absolutely took off as soon as it was published.

I fulfilled a lifelong dream of becoming a bestselling author. I experienced my first fans (NEVER gets old!!) and for more than a decade, I received letters from women all over the world, who thanked me for helping them find their soulmates.

I began teaching classes and coaching, which has become one of the biggest joys of my life. I've met hundreds of fascinating people in green rooms all over the world, because of my book. I got to do some very cool stuff with some fascinating people

— like the time I was the real-life dating expert on the HITCH movie featurette and DVD starring Will Smith, or another time I was halfway around the world in London and a complete stranger recognized me from the photo on my book cover, or the time I was a magazine cover girl.

Not to mention, it landed me a weekly gig as the on-air relationships expert on a national morning TV show for more than 15 years, which I absolutely loved. Seriously, some of the coolest, most creative, most interesting people I've ever met in my life.

*Me, co-hosting NBC's DAYTIME show*

All of that, because of a book that took me just a few weeks to write.

My first book opened up a world of opportunities for me and changed my life. Just as I hope *this book*, and *your own book*, will change yours.

## Does this sound like you?

This book is for you if:

- You want to write a self-help book to grow your business and your audience – and you have something valuable to teach the world

- You know what you want to say but don't know exactly how to put it in book form

- You may have already tried to write a book yourself, but got stuck and you don't know how to get unstuck

- You don't know where to start, or you're struggling to get over the finish line

- You're in a time crunch and need to get a book done quickly for a specific event or launch timeline

- You're already super busy –and you're wondering when you'll possibly find the time to write a whole book

- You want it done yesterday

- You want to write a book that is structured to build your business (build your newsletter list, sell higher priced offerings, position you as an authority/expert on your topic) but aren't sure how to do that without being salesy and obnoxious

## Why you need to publish a self-help book

If you, like Theodora, have an incredible idea for a book, or a concept you want to share with the world, this book will help you do just that.

After all, writing a self-help book is one of the most effective methods to build your reputation, establish your authority in your niche, attract new clients and customers, charge more for your services, gain paid speaking opportunities, build your newsletter list, and upsell your more expensive offerings, including courses, retreats and conferences, mastermind groups, and even one-on-one coaching.

But writing a book can be daunting if you don't know what you're doing, or if you have no one to guide you.

Are you feeling completely overwhelmed when you think about writing your book? Frustrated? Stressed out?

I can relate -- I see it every day with my book-coaching clients and Bestseller Academy students.

**It's true. Writing a self-help book can be an exasperating, time-wasting endeavor if you've never written one before. (And sometimes, even if you have!)**

- How do you avoid the biggest mistakes writers make when writing a non-fiction book?

- How do you write a self-help book if you're a coach or business pro, but *not really a writer*?

- How can you build your book in such a way that it naturally builds your email list, and drives customers and clients to your other higher-priced offerings?

- How can you write a book you're actually proud of?

- What are the elements you *must have* in your non-fiction book? And in *what order*?

- How do you write a self-help book that actually empowers and helps the people you're trying to help?

It's not always as easy as it seems at first glance – especially when you don't quite have a handle on what you're doing yet.

## You've got this

The good news is that you can do this -- even if you've never written a book before.

Even if you've written dozens of books and you just want to get better.

How? By using my **Bestseller Academy Blueprint.**

The Blueprint is the exact same step-by-step formula I use with both my first-time authors *and* my six and seven-figure author coaching students.

## Hi! I'm Lisa, a bestselling author and book coach

I'm Lisa Daily. In case you were wondering, I'm a *USA Today* bestselling, award-winning self-help and fiction author and book coach with 20+ years of experience in both traditional publishing and self-publishing, and my published students include both **first-time authors** and ***USA Today* bestselling authors** who earn over seven figures a year. (And everyone in between.)

In addition to being an internationally bestselling self-help author myself, I've coached some of the biggest names in the business, including Renee Rose (*Write to Riches*), Skye Warren (*The Bestselling Author Next Door*), Theodora Taylor (*7-Figure Fiction*), Maggie Marr (*Books to Film and TV*), Heather Hildenbrand (Manifest *Your HEA*), Lee Savino (*Adventures with the Universe*), Kel Carpenter (*Rule Your Authordom*), Vanessa Vale, and many others.

My step-by-step **Bestseller Academy Blueprint** is a proven strategy that I have personally used as an award-winning, bestselling self-help author, and with my book coaching students to write their bestselling self-help and non-fiction books quickly and confidently – even when they've never written a book before.

I'll show you exactly what you need to know to quickly and easily write your own self-help book, and avoid costly and frustrating mistakes.

**By the end of this book you will learn:**

- How to write your self-help book step-by-step in just 2 weeks!

- How to structure your self-help book in a way that makes your content resonate and helps readers best learn the lessons you want to teach them

- The BIGGEST MISTAKE most first-time authors make (that makes you look like a JERK!) and how to avoid it

- How to avoid costly and frustrating mistakes most first-time nonfiction authors make

- How to build reader magnets into your book so you

can grow your mailing list effortlessly

- Secret strategies to make your book more appealing to both readers and the media, and

- How to easily upsell your readers your courses and coaching – baked right into the book.

I know you can write a self-help book. You just need someone to show you the way.

And that's why I'm here. And I'll be with you through every single chapter until you reach "The End."

Ready to finally write that book you've been dreaming of?

Let's get started.

## Chapter 2

# The Struggle is Real. But Not Inevitable.

It may (or may not) surprise you to learn that I also initially struggled with writing my first self-help book.

I was an advertising copywriter with a new baby, and a brief window in which to launch a new career as an author (aka maternity leave.) I did not want to go back to working in an office. I wanted to stay at home making googly eyes with my squishy, adorable little baby all day, but still earn a living and exercise my brain. I was on a mission.

**I also had no idea what I was doing.**

Like many of us, I started my search for answers at the bookstore. Unfortunately, after reading almost a dozen books, I just couldn't find what I needed.

Certainly, there were books that purported to teach an aspiring author how to write a non-fiction or self-help book, but they were often written by agents or publishers or others who didn't have any experience *actually writing* self-help books. Most of them contained a number of general and unhelpful platitudes such as, "Figure out what you want to write about" and "Write every day".

Well, *great*.

I had figured out what I wanted to write *about*, But how was I going to write every day when I had no idea *what* I was supposed to be writing, or *how* I was supposed to be writing it?

How was I supposed to start my self-help book? What did it need to include? Why didn't my early attempt *feel* like a real book?

I was looking for specifics — a step-by-step plan to help me structure and write my first self-help book. And I was stuck.

I began researching bestselling self-help books in my particular genre, dating advice, and compiling data on the elements they had in common. Then, I expanded my research to all types of self-help. I also researched self-help books that weren't selling particularly well to see what they had in common as well.

## You know what I discovered?

The most popular self-help books had many similar and important elements that the poorly selling self-help books did not. The bestselling and most-reviewed self-help books also included many of the best practices of instructional design, meaning they were specifically built in a way to best help the reader most effectively learn the information the author was presenting.

But there was more. The top-selling self-help books also managed to form a deeper connection with the readers themselves.

## Eureka!

Once I knew all the elements my book should include, it became a lot easier to write it. I just reverse-engineered what was already working for other self-help authors. I wrote my first self-help book, *Stop Getting Dumped!* in just six weeks, 2-3 hours a day while my baby was napping. And despite the fact that I had no platform to speak of and was a first-time author, I received offers from all six (at the time) New York publishing houses. **That book became an international bestseller.**

Fast forward several years and more than ten books later, I've taught hundreds of authors just like you exactly what they need to do to structure and write a self-help book, quickly and easily. Some, like Theodora, are experienced bestselling authors with a massive fan base. Others have never written a book before.

And no matter where you are on your publishing journey, I can teach you too.

You have something important to say, and I want to make sure you have every tool you need to get your self-help book out into the world.

So grab your laptop, and let's get started.

If you're planning to write your self-help book in 14 days, here's the schedule you'll need to follow:

> **14-Day Book Completion Schedule**
> DAY 1: Complete Creative Work Plan
> DAY 2: Brainstorm book titles and plan names
> DAY 3: Write chapters one and two
> DAY 4 - 11: Write Action Plan chapters
> DAY 12: Write Troubleshooting (FAQ), Future and Beyond, Contact Info chapter
> DAY 13: Write Resources chapter
> DAY 14: Create readers magnets, set up email platform, add links to text and Resources Section of your book

**Your first step? Block off time in your calendar this week specifically for writing. Adding it to your calendar lets your brain know that writing this book is important to you and you'll do what you need to do in order to get it finished.**

Be sure to set reminders on your phone before your writing time to get your brain ready to write.

**Want an inspirational 14-day daily pep talk as you write your book? I've got you covered!**

**Sign up for 2 weeks of daily motivation in your inbox here.**

*Open the camera app on your phone to click the QR code to get 2 weeks of daily pep talks & tips to help you stay on track and finish your book.*

**Note:** Obviously, if you can only block off 15 minutes a day for writing, it will more than likely take you longer than 14 days to finish your book. That said, if you follow the steps in this book and write at a medium pace of 2,000 - 3,000 words per day, you'll be able to complete your 20K - 40K word self-help book in approximately 14 days.

If you are able to, schedule the same time every day, maybe an hour or two in the morning before you start your regular workday (#5amwritersclub is a thing!).

Could you build some time into your existing work schedule, or maybe dedicate a few hours each night to writing your book after your house settles down for the evening?

Blocking off writing time on your calendar and sticking to it is a key component to successfully writing your book.

If it's not possible given your existing schedule to dedicate several hours a day to writing your nonfiction book, work with what you have.

- Can you spare 30 minutes today?

- Can you write and eat lunch at the same time?

- Can you dictate your self-help book on the train as you commute to your day job?

- Or in the school pick-up line? (Trust me, you will not be the first or even the hundredth author to write a book while waiting in the carpool lane or sitting in the bleachers at swim practice.) I personally dictated sections of this book while driving a usually-boring, isolated stretch of highway on a 4-hour car trip.

Setting time aside every day to write will help you build momentum, and as any author will tell you, when it comes to writing a book, momentum is your greatest friend.

Let's build some!

## WRITE NOW: Bestseller Book Building Blocks

To write a self-help book you need to:
- **Dedicate time to write.** Right now, go ahead and mark off time in your calendar to write

for the next 14 days. It can be as little as 30 minutes, or as much as 8 hours (long day!), but make that time commitment right now. Be sure to set yourself reminders on your phone or digital calendar to remind you to write before each session. That literal reminder will help your new writing habit stick.

- **Workbook:** If you're the type of person who likes to keep all your notes organized and in one place (and, you know, *pretty,*) I've created an awesome workbook to go along with this book, just for you. Not the workbook type? No worries, you'll be able to download any PDFs or documents you'll need to write your book along the way.

- **Create a new manuscript document** using Google Docs (free!), ButterDocs, or similar writing program. (You can [download a Google Doc template here](#) with both the Creative Work Plan and Bestseller Academy Blueprint.)

- **Bonus:** To make the most of your self-help book for business-building purposes, you'll also need an email platform, such as [MailerLite](#) or MailChimp. You can get up and running with just the free plan.

That's it! My Bestseller Academy Blueprint will do all the heavy lifting for you. All you need to do is follow the outline step-by-step, and dedicate time every day or week to write your book.

## Chapter 3

# Your Secret Weapon! The Creative Work Plan

As I mentioned earlier, I actually come from an advertising background. I was a copywriter for several years before I started writing books, And it makes for an excellent training ground for authors.

In advertising, before you ever start writing a commercial or radio spot or a print ad or online ad, you always start with a creative brief, or work plan.

The creative brief is a document that you use to really help to drill down on what's important, who you're talking to and what you're going to say to them.

**Why does this matter?**

Because part of the reason it is so challenging (and we get stuck when writing) a self-help book is that we often do not think about the reader, their problems, their pain points, what we offer to make it all better, or what makes us different from every other person out there with a self-help book on our specific topic. (And believe me – whatever you want to write about – there are *a lot*.)

Instead, we think about what *we* want to say. What *we* want to share. What will help *us* grow our businesses.

Don't get me wrong, all of those things are important to think about too. But none of them are really that important to your reader. They're reading your book, they're coming to you, because they have a problem that *they* need to solve, or something that is causing the pain or distress in *their* life, and they hope you are the person to help them solve it.

**BESTSELLER ACADEMY
EXTRA CREDIT
If you want your book to be successful, if you want to change people's lives for the better, you need to focus on your reader.**

Think about this: As you're reading this book, do you care about my plans to grow my business? Or do you care how I can help you to write your own self-help book? *Exactly.*

Your readers are buying your book to solve their own problems, exactly as they should.

The details in the Creative Work Plan are ones that we need to be incredibly clear on before we ever start writing the book. Now, if you are reading this book after having made several attempts to structure your self-help book on your own, do not worry.

Clarifying the information in the Creative Work Plan help you to get back on track with your nonfiction book. It is the secret sauce that makes your book connect with your readers on a deeper level, solves their problem(s), and leaves them feeling empowered and grateful to the person (YOU!) who made them feel that way.

> **That's our goal here: to solve people's problems, to take away their pain and frustration, to make life (or dating, or publishing a book, or eating clean, or learning how to knit) easier for them to manage with the tools and strategies we've worked hard to figure out.**

Your self-help book will make the world better. Because it will change someone's (or hopefully, many someones) life for the better.

That's one heck of a mission in life. And I'm positive you're up to the task.

> **Taadaa! My Creative Work Plan**
> 1. Key Fact
> 2. Problem the Book Must Solve
> 3. Objective of the Book
> 4. The Strategy
> 5. Your Prime Reader
> 6. Your Reader's Pain Points
> 7. Positioning
> 8. Promise
> 9. Reason Why

## Grab Your Workbook (or Notebook) and Let's Break Down My Creative Work Plan

You can download a fillable G-doc of my Creative Work Plan here: https://hello.lisadailybooks.com/write-a-self-help-book-free-resources

## 1. Key Fact

**What is the single most important fact upon which your book can have an effect?**

We're going to kick things off here by figuring out exactly why your reader might seek out your book in the first place. The **Key Fact** is something that is generally universally true for your target reader.

**Key Fact examples for different types of books:**

a. (This book!) Many people, including writers, coaches, and entrepreneurs, would like to write a self-help book but don't know how.

b. (Dating advice) It hurts to get dumped.

c. (Business book) Starting a new business has a high failure rate and can be really expensive.

What's your Key Fact?

## 2. Problem the Book Must Solve

In this section, think about the following: What does the reader need?

Examples for different types of books:

a. The reader needs a step-by-step blueprint to turn their ideas into a book that will serve their audiences and their businesses.

b. The reader needs a dating strategy to help them avoid heartbreak and meet "the one."

c. The reader needs a guide for how to structure and start a home-based business for less than $500

See how the **Key Fact** and the **Problem the Book Must Solve** work together?

What's the problem the book must solve for your reader?
How is it impacted by your key fact?

## 3. Objective of the Book

What effect will this book have on the reader's life?
Examples for different types of books:

a. This book will teach readers to write a self-help book to build their business – confidently and quickly while avoiding common mistakes.

b. This book will help readers finally find "the one".

c. This book will show readers exactly how to structure/start their own home-based business so they can avoid costly mistakes and finally gain control of their own finances and work life

Your book is the solution to the reader's problem. What will it do for them?

## 4. The Strategy

What are the specifics of how you will achieve the **Objective of the Book** (#3) that will solve the reader's **Problem** (#2)? This is the place to outline your step-by-step plan of action for your reader.

Example:

My step-by-step plan is a proven strategy that I have personally used as a bestselling author, and that my book coaching students have used to write their own bestselling self-help and non-fiction books quickly and confidently – even when they've never written a book before.

1. *Complete Lisa's Creative Work Plan*

2. *Write your chapters following the Bestseller Academy*

*Blueprint. Note – the Blueprint itself is the key component of the strategy.*

3. *Review your manuscript for reader magnet and Resources opportunities.*

4. *Decide if you want to also create a workbook to go along with your book. (Workbooks are extremely helpful for readers, helping them separate the strategy to accomplish their goals from the tactics they'll need to do so.)*

5. *Create your workbook*

6. *Create your reader magnets.*

7. *Choose your best publishing option and launch your book and/or workbook!*

## 5. Your Prime Reader

Who is the ideal reader & buyer of this book?

Include demographic, psychographic, and other research or info you have about your target audience.

If you're a coach or entrepreneur, you're in luck! Just think about the demographics (age, income, etc) and pain points (What's keeping them from getting what they want? What are they already paying you to solve?) of your existing clients.

What do you know about them as a group?

Example:

- College Educated or Some college
- Entrepreneur/ coach/influencer/writer
- Time-crunched
- Wants to write a book to expand her business
- May or may not take a utilitarian approach to writing
- Feels lost or out of her depth when thinking about writing a book, or wants the process to go as quickly and smoothly as possible
- M/F but skews female
- Income level: middle/upper; upper

**Prime Reader Example:**

My ideal reader is a coach, entrepreneur, writer, or influencer (some are all 4). She's looking to scale up her business, become an authority in her space, make some money, or have something to give or sell to her coaching clients.

She's an educated, successful, smart, entrepreneur or thought leader. She finds value in coaching/learning and may be a coach herself. She has a unique perspective to offer others, and needs help getting it out into the world in book form.

As a busy entrepreneur, she values her limited time and will invest in books, services, courses, and coaching in order to accomplish her goals more quickly, easily, effectively, and efficiently.

She realizes that writing a book makes an excellent strategy to grow her business via higher-priced courses, speaking engagements, one-on-one coaching, and more.

She's likely got some resources, is 30-60, college educated, and she's entrepreneurial-minded.

## **Create an avatar of your prime reader**

If you're unfamiliar, an avatar is a representation of a person or group. In the process of completing the Creative Work Plan for your book, you'll either choose someone you know (easiest!) or create an imaginary person to put a "face" to your readers.

Your avatar will serve as a touchstone throughout the writing process.

### **How to create your reader avatar**

Your avatar is where you take that demographic data from your Prime Reader Example (above) and create an imaginary person (or think of a real one you know) that fits within your reader parameters.

Why do we do this? Because it's easier to drill down to what's important when you're thinking about how you would address a single person.

Some of my authors actually have a specific client in mind as they are writing their books, and that can be really helpful as you write. I wrote my first book, *Stop Getting Dumped!*, with my good friend Tina in mind, and I still use real people as my self-help avatars whenever I have a chance.

Why? Because a real person gives you more pushback against your ideas, which is super helpful. If I know someone in real life, I know the kind of behaviors my avatar/friend has that are sabotaging their goals. I know what they're telling me and themselves about their situation that keeps them stuck where they are. And I know from talking to them exactly why they are coming to me for my help.

That said, if you're just starting out with coaching and/or you don't have a specific person in mind, you can just make up an imaginary person. Add enough detail to make him/her feel realistic so you can really imagine them when you're thinking about addressing their problems, challenges, and pain points.

Later, as you're writing, you'll rely on this real or imaginary person for help when you're addressing your reader's concerns, obstacles, and the surprises along the way that are most likely to trip them up.

This also helps to keep your writing centered on the single reader's experience. **She'll feel like you're talking directly to her, helping her to solve her problems.** This is a much different experience than when a book reads like it's been aimed at a crowd, (aka no one in particular.)

When you create this imaginary person, it helps you to really understand your reader before you ever start writing your book.

**Here's an avatar example:**

*My reader avatar is Bethany. She's 41 years old, college educated, and owns a wellness coaching business. She's scaling her business this year and wants to write a book to give herself an advantage over her competitors in the space. She may also develop a course or product line on the same topic. When she tried writing it on her own she felt lost and stuck – and realized she needed some guidance to say what she wants to say. She's still in her bootstrapping phase, and is either a one-woman show or working with a virtual assistant, so time is tight and her most valuable resource. She knows writing a non-fiction book will give her credibility and help her land more big-dollar clients, so she's making a time and financial commitment to write and publish her book. She discovered my book while searching online for answers.*

**Here's another reader avatar example for this book:**

*My reader avatar is Liz. She's a 45-year-old, seven-figure romance author who wants to write a writing craft book to help other authors achieve her level of success. While she's very comfortable writing fiction, she feels out of her depth writing self-help. She frequently hires coaches to help her level up in her business, and she found me via my YouTube video on how to structure a self-help book. She's confident in her writing skills, but not in writing non-fiction. She does not have time to waste fooling around and figuring things out. She may be planning to roll out the book along with a course on the same topic, or in conjunction with a talk she's planning to give at a writers' conference.*

You only need one, but I wanted to give you a couple of different examples because your avatar doesn't need to be perfect – she just needs to feel like a person so that when you get stuck periodically as you are writing your book, you can think back to your avatar and **her needs**.

She's the person you're writing the book for, and you want to make sure she gets everything out of your book that you've promised her – and more.

As I'm writing this book, I'm thinking about *you*. How can I make this writing process easier on you? How can I give you the very best odds of successfully writing and publishing your self-help book? What are some of the challenges I can help you overcome?

> **If you constantly keep your reader in mind, you will write a book that matters. A book that changes lives. And that's all any of us can hope for.**

## Think about this: How do you solve your reader avatar's problems?

What does Bethany need in order to successfully write her book with the intention of growing her business? What are

Bethany's pain points? How will she respond to the advice I'm giving her? How can I make this easier on her?

## 6. Determine Your Reader's Pain Points

A pain point is a part of a process, system, or experience that causes your reader or customer problems or obstructions.

What are your reader's pain points? Why is not knowing this information causing her trouble/pain in her life?

> **Your pain point is something that stops or hinders you from achieving your goals.**

Because you're reading *this* book, I know that your goal is to write a self-help book. Because I work with many new and experienced authors to write their first self-help books, I'm aware of (and skilled at overcoming) all of the barriers and obstacles to success they might face.

For example:

- Writing a book takes time, and you're very busy

- You don't want to waste time

- You got stuck trying to write a book yourself

- You know what you want to say but don't know exactly how to put it in book form.

- You need to get a book done quickly for a specific event or launch timeline.

- You want to write a book that is structured to build your business (build your newsletter list, sell higher priced offerings, position you as an authority/expert on your topic) but don't want to be salesy and obnoxious.

Can you relate to any of these pain points? Which ones? (Don't worry, we're going to solve for all of them as we make our way through this book.)

What are your reader's (or coaching clients') pain points? They're paying you because they've come to a point in the process where they can't move on to the next step without help – they need *you* to help them solve their problem (or problems or overcome the obstacles that are standing in their way.)

**Write those down**, because solving them for your readers is what will make them love you, tell all their friends and peers how awesome you are, and keep buying your books and courses.

## 7. Positioning

Define the market *category* for your book, as well as the *segment* in which your book will compete. What is the reason your book needs to exist? What can it offer your prime reader that no one else's book does?

Example:

Self-Help/Writing & Publishing Advice

An easy way to figure this out is by thinking about where you would locate your book in the bookstore. For self-help, there are numerous potential categories, including:

- Happiness

- Relationships

- Success

- Money

- Spiritual

- Stress Management

- Memory Improvement

- Self-Esteem

- Relaxation

Where does your book belong?

**Segment:**

Which groups specifically is your book written for?

This book is written for entrepreneurs, coaches, influencers, fiction authors, and other aspiring authors.

Which groups is your book targeting? Online daters? Wellness seekers? Entrepreneurs?

**The reason your book needs to exist:**

Why does your book need to exist? What does it provide that other options don't?

Sometimes, the difference is your perspective or approach. For example, I'm not only a bestselling self-help author myself, but I also do book coaching for students ranging from brand new authors to some incredibly successful 6- and 7-figure authors. This unique perspective is why <u>this</u> book needs to exist.

Here's an example:

**This book needs to exist because:**
- Many coaches & entrepreneurs want to write a book to grow their influence, grow their business, and make more money, BUT there are very few step-by-step

resources to get them over the finish line.

- Few non-fiction writing books are written by USA Today bestselling authors who have successfully written self-help books

- There are very few books that show readers exactly how to structure a self-help book step-by-step.

- Most "how to write a book" books are not written for professionals/coaches who want to write a book for a specific purpose

- My book will offer a roadmap for those both interested in self-publishing and traditional publishing.

- I am a six-figure author coach who is a bestselling author myself and have coached numerous bestselling authors (and also new/aspiring authors)

- My readers are afraid of what happens if they fail to write a book — they'll waste time of money, their competitors will overtake them, they won't be able to scale their business

Sometimes there isn't any other book in the market that teaches your audience what they're trying to learn. (If you happen to know how to play a hammer dulcimer, please publish your book TODAY. I will pre-order that sucker the second you put it up on Amazon.)

Sometimes the book needs to exist because your method of doing something is different than everyone else's. Or if it's similar, you've successfully branded your method to make it seem unique even if it's not.

What makes your book different from the other books that are similar to yours?

Give these questions some serious consideration, because figuring out what makes your book unique in a sea of sameness will be the very factor that makes your book a must-read for your audience (and a key component of your marketing efforts.)

**Start with this question: What can I offer my reader that no one else's book does?**

This is a tough one, but it's critical to understanding exactly what it is that you have to offer your reader.

Example:

-I'm a traditionally published author, and also an indie author (both worlds)

-I'm an internationally bestselling self-help author

**-I'm a non-fiction coach for other 6- and 7-figure bestselling authors**

-I'm a self-help book coach for hundreds of first-time authors

-My plan helps authors at every stage write the best self-help book they can, and shows them to use their book as a tool to grow their business.

While these are all good offerings, the one that is *most unique to me* is the fact that bestselling and mega-bestselling authors come to me to coach them through writing their non-fiction books.

What can **you** offer your reader that no one else's book does?

## 8. Promise

What is the <u>very best argument</u> for why the reader should buy your book?

Example: This book will teach you the proven method to quickly and easily write a self-help book in 14 days, and avoid costly and frustrating mistakes.

**Be specific about what you're promising your reader.** Don't just tell them you'll help them earn more money. Tell them you'll show them **how** to earn 6 figures.

When I'm thinking about my promise to the reader, I complete this sentence: **"By the time you finish reading this book, you will learn..."**

Like this:

By the time you finish this book, you will learn:

- How to write your non-fiction or self-help book

step-by-step

- How to structure your self-help book so your readers can learn from you

- How to avoid costly and frustrating mistakes most first-time nonfiction authors make

- How to build reader magnets into your book so you can grow your mailing list effortlessly

- The BIGGEST MISTAKE most first-time authors make, and how to avoid it

- Secret strategies to make your book more appealing to readers and the media

- How to easily upsell your readers your courses and coaching – baked right into the book.

- Everything you need to know to successfully write your self-help book in as few as 2 weeks

I love to start with a "By the time you finish reading this book, you will learn…" statement or bullet list because it helps to really drill down what it is you'll be teaching your reader.

In addition, this question is super critical because you will most likely use it, or a variation of it, in both your marketing copy for the book as well as in the beginning section of the book.

I LOVE this section because it really forces you to think about the specific information you'll be imparting to your reader. It makes it easier for your target reader to determine if yours is the book they need (yes!) and easier for both of you to ensure the reader is getting everything out of the book that they were promised.

Earlier in the Creative Work Plan (Step 6) I asked you to write down your reader's pain points – the things that are stopping them from achieving their goals: **Make sure that you include solutions to your reader's pain points in your promise!**

Once you've filled in the blanks on the "By the time you finish this book you will learn..." sentence and come up with several options, look at all of the various promises you've written down and choose the one that *best solves* your reader's pain points. **That is your primary promise.**

You'll use that promise to build your book's subtitle, and it will serve as your north star as you are writing the book.

## 9. Reason Why

WHY does your book deliver this promise to the reader? What is the SUPPORT for your promise? Can you keep it?

Example:

My book delivers the promise to the reader because not only am I a bestselling self-help author myself, but I have also taught hundreds of other authors from newbie to 7-figures how to successfully write a self-help book.

Brainstorm to find your best "Reasons Why", like this:

- I'm a USA TODAY bestselling author myself, with 20+ years in publishing

- I have helped thousands of aspiring authors to 7-figure bestselling authors to write their self-help books.

- Numerous coaching client books have hit the bestseller list

- **7-Figure bestselling authors choose me to coach them through writing their non-fiction books.**

- I'm a hybrid (both traditionally published and indie-published) internationally bestselling author myself

- I know exactly where aspiring self-help authors get stuck (and how to get them unstuck) because I see it over and over again in my book coaching practice and Bestseller Academy Courses

- Support: Private coaching students are prestigious and write glowing testimonials

Can I keep the promise? Yes! I can keep that promise!

Can you keep your promise(s) to your reader? Heck yeah, you can.

## WRITE NOW: Bestseller Book Building Blocks

**Complete the Creative Work Plan.** To get started, grab your workbook or download your free copy of my Creative Work Plan here: https://hello.lisadailybooks.com/write-a-self-help-book-free-resources

This will help you to drill down and identify who your reader is, the problem you're trying to solve for them, and exactly how you're going to do that, step by step.

Once you've got that figured out, you'll be ready to move to the next step!

## Chapter 4

# Brainstorming Your Catchy, Benefit-Driven Title & Action Plan Name

When you think about the title for your new book, you may already have some idea in your mind. Unfortunately most first-time self-help authors come up with the title that resonates with them personally, rather than searching for a title that will both be easily found by, and resonate with, their target reader.

> **Staying focused on *what the reader needs* versus *what you want* can be one of the more**

**challenging aspects of writing a self-help book.**

# Brainstorming your title & plan name

As you begin writing your self help book, you're going to need to come up with a **plan name** for your program or method to help your reader solve their problem.

Examples of this include:

*The Bestseller Academy Blueprint*

*The 4-Hour Work Week*

*The HEA Method*

*The Atkins Diet*

*1 Year to 6 Figures*

It's a really good idea to come up with your plan name before you start thinking about your book title. One reason for this is that sometimes your plan name is so strong that it also works as your book title. (*The 4-Hour Work Week, Fit and Fabulous in 15 Minutes.*)

## Your plan name is just as important as your book title, maybe more

Why is your plan name so important? Because it's the powerful and easy-to-remember language your readers will use when they're talking about your book or method with other people they know and on social media.

One of the worst things you can do as an author is not give your reader an easy way to discuss your book with others.

That's why it's so critical to come up with a memorable plan name and/or title. A great plan name helps to sell more books – and better still, it helps you build your brand so that when you're ready to offer courses, coaching, or other products you'll already have a method people have heard of.

Your book can be a rockstar when it comes to building your business, if you do it right.

Giving your plan an awesome name promotes "group speak", which is the language members of a certain in-group (like members of the military, authors, or YouTubers) use to speak to each other.

Remember my client Theodora Taylor, the bestselling author of *7-Figure Fiction*? Her overarching idea/plan is called Universal Fantasy which she refers to throughout the book as "butter". Since the day *7-Figure Fiction* was published, it's been nearly impossible to attend a writing conference without hearing authors talk about adding "butter" to their books. That's the power of an awesome plan name.

Bonus: Be sure to give your plan name or title more power by referring to it frequently throughout your book.


## Your book's title should be a crystal-clear promise to your reader

First, your title needs to communicate to the reader <u>what the book is about</u>.
Second, it needs to clearly communicate <u>the benefit to the reader.</u>

How do you accomplish this? **Put a clear promise on the cover of your book.**

My first (bestselling) book was entitled *Stop Getting Dumped!* This is a strong title because it's easy to remember, clearly communicates that it's a dating advice book, and the benefit (no longer being dumped) is extremely valuable to my ideal reader, someone who has struggled to meet "the one".

*Stop Getting Dumped!* is a clear promise. So is *Write a Self-help Book in 14 Days*

Not to mention:

*Build the Life You Want*
*The Dopamine Detox*
*How to Win Friends and Influence People*
*How to Be the Love You Seek*
*You Can Negotiate Anything*
*You Are a Badass at Making Money*
*How to Talk to Anyone*
*Think Faster, Talk Smarter*
*Decluttering at the Speed of Life*
*Write to Riches*
*Manifest Your HEA*
*Be Happier By Tomorrow*

The reader absolutely knows what they're getting. If winning friends, making more money, finding love, or writing a book is the reader's goal, your title lets them know they've come to the right place.

Now, while I absolutely love it when your book's plan name works as a title, this is not always the case. For example, in this book, the plan name is the **Bestseller Academy Blueprint.** It's a bit fuzzier on the benefits as a book title than I generally prefer, although it does communicate some benefit to the reader through the use of the words "bestseller" and "blueprint"

The word "bestseller" clearly communicates that the method I'm teaching you has been used by bestselling authors to write bestselling books. That's a big benefit!

The word "blueprint" communicates that the process is proven and relatively straightforward, and better still, that there are specific steps for the reader (you!) to achieve success.

But even though that is the plan name, it's a bit challenging as a title. For one thing, the major online bookseller (who shall go unnamed) rarely allows the word "bestseller" or "bestselling" in a book title, even when the author can prove that they are in fact a bestselling author. Personally, I don't like to borrow trouble, so it's easier to just go ahead and choose a different title.

Secondly, we have the opportunity to add in some additional benefits if I use another title. With *Write a Self-Help Book in 14 Days*, for example, I've added in another key reader benefit — you can use my process to write a book in just 14 days! In two weeks, you can be an author! So in addition to the benefits in the plan name (bestseller, blueprint) I've also added a relatively short timeframe, which is another critical benefit for my readers. (Finish writing your book in 14 days! Woohoo!)

## About book titles

Before you get started, I want to say a few things about titling your book.

First, coming up with a great title is an entirely different skill set than writing a book or coaching, or a million other things. Many talented authors find it a struggle to come up with a good title. If you happen to be one of them, don't feel too badly about it.

This is solvable. Don't let it worry you.

The great thing about nonfiction is that while a very clever title can certainly help you sell books and charm readers, a book with a fairly simple, benefit-driven title, can hit the bestseller list as well. In fact, if you have to choose between the two, I would take a strong benefit-driven title over a clever one every day of the week.

Of course, the Holy Grail is when you can manage to do both. Two of my favorites are *The 4-Hour Workweek* by Tim Ferriss and *Fit and Fabulous in 15 Minutes* by Teresa Tapp.

*Sidebar: I'm wondering what this says about me that these are two of my favorite book titles... I guess it says I would like to have exercised and be done with work by noon every day, haha.*

Here are some things to keep in mind, while coming up with the title for your book:

**1. After you complete your Creative Work Plan, make a list of 20 to 40 potential Action Plan names for your book.**

Let your mind wander and write down anything that comes into your brain. Some of them will be crap. Okay, most of them will be crap. That's okay. The crap titles get your brain humming along for the good stuff. And some of them will be awesome. (Hopefully at least one of your ideas would make a great title for your book.) Sometimes you come up with a great idea on the very first try, but you won't know that that is the best idea until you've gone through the exercise and written down another 29 possibilities.

Back in the day when I worked in advertising, I would write anywhere from 20 to 100 variations on a headline. The same strategy works well for titles and Action Plan names.

**2. Repeat the exercise for your book titles, and write down 20–40 potential options.**

**3. If you don't have a great idea for a title ▫after you do the exercise of writing down at least 20 title**

**possibilities, choose the best one as a *working title*, and continue on with the process of writing your book.**

We don't want to get stuck on our title, especially because an awesome title often bubbles up while we're writing. Choose the one that is closest to what you want to say. You can always go back later and substitute in the final title or plan name once the book is written.

## 4. Keep your list of potential titles in your workbook, on a separate document, or in the notes app on your phone.

Once you start thinking about potential titles for your book, you'll find you keep getting ideas for them while you're doing other things... Driving the car, taking a shower, loading the dishwasher. Make sure to write them down as soon as they enter your brain so that you don't lose them. This is especially important if you think of a title right as you're falling asleep, or wake up from a dream with a spectacularly good title idea that you are positive is so awesome you will remember it in the morning. **You won't.**

Please trust me and every other author who has fallen into the same trap. You *won't remember it in the morning*. Chances are, it may be perfect. Or, it may be completely nonsensical. I always keep a notebook by my bed for these middle of the night thoughts, and sometimes an entire chapter of a book comes fully formed from my brain at 2 am. And sometimes I wake up in the morning to a bit of odd chicken scratch on my notepad that reads something like *ketchup (squeeze bottle ONLY!) + bicycle helmet =awesome sauce.* (With no context or memory whatsoever.)

Creating a memorable title for your plan and book is essential for attracting readers and making a lasting impression.

## Address your reader's pain points with your book's subtitle

While self-help titles are typically splashy and attention grabbing, self-help book *subtitles* generally include a specific description of what readers can expect from the book.

Review your answer from the Creative Work Plan, question #9, where you created a primary promise to your reader – the one that best solves your reader's pain points.

Use that promise to build your book's subtitle.

Example: My readers' pain points are that they want to write a self-help book, and don't know where to start, or how to structure it. They've likely struggled for a while, trying to figure it out on their own, and have now come to the conclusion they need help.

My subtitle: *The proven, step-by-step plan to easily write your non-fiction book – from the bestselling author coach*

Do you see how my subtitle directly addresses my readers' biggest sources of pain and frustration?

> **BESTSELLER ACADEMY**
> **EXTRA CREDIT**
> **You'll notice that many of the most successful subtitles make a promise to the reader. Review the reader promise from your Creative Work Plan – can you turn your promise into a succinct subtitle?**

For example:

*Stop Getting Dumped!: All You Need to Know to Make Men Fall Madly in Love with You and Marry "The One" in 3 Years or Less*

*Atomic Habits: An Easy & Proven Way to Build Good Habits & Break Bad Ones*

*Dopamine Detox: A Short Guide to Remove Distractions and Get Your Brain to Do Hard Things*

*Hidden Potential: The Science of Achieving Greater Things*

*The Courage to Be Disliked: The Japanese Phenomenon That Shows You How to Change Your Life and Achieve Real Happiness*

*Attached: The New Science of Adult Attachment and How It Can Help You Find—and Keep—Love*

**The subtitle and title work together to grab the reader's attention (title), and tell them why they need your book to solve their problem. (subtitle)**

If you are SEO-savvy, you can go one step further and give your book title or subtitle an online advantage by taking a look at the phrasing of your reader promise, and tweaking it to align with desirable search phrases and long-tail keywords.

If you do decide to incorporate some SEO into your subtitle, be sure the phrasing feels natural and meant for human readers. You don't want to give your book a spammy feel right on the cover. Ultimately, you'll want to remember that it will be a real, live, human person who will be reading your book.

If you do it right, you'll be building a long-term relationship with your reader – and you really don't want to get off on the wrong foot.

## Some powerful self-help title strategies

Below you'll find a few popular naming strategies to consider as you brainstorm titles and subtitles for your book.

## Address the reader directly

The most effective format for a self-help book is writing it in second person (you/we) as though you are having a one-on-one conversation with the reader. As I'm writing this, I'm just thinking about YOU, and how I can help you write your self-help book. I'm addressing you as though we are having a one-on-one chat over lunch, coffee, or Zoom, like I do with my one-on-one book coaching students.

Great news! This is not only the most effective format for writing a self-help book – but also, it's a pretty effective strategy for titling as well.

People pay more attention to information that affects them directly, and a direct address in your title shows your reader right on the cover – THIS BOOK IS FOR YOU.

Some great examples include:

*You Are a Badass at Making Money: Master the Mindset of Wealth* by Jen Sincero

*What Happened to You?: Conversations on Trauma, Resilience, and Healing* by Oprah Winfrey & Bruce D. Perry

*You Can Negotiate Anything: How to Get What You Want* by Herb Cohen

*You Can Heal Your Life* By Louise Hay

## Inspire the reader

Some of the most successful self-help book titles inspire the reader with the compelling magic of what is *possible*. Inspiring titles typically make some big promises around happiness, growth, money, or love.

Some examples include:

*Big Magic* by Elizabeth Gilbert

*Million Dollar Habits: 27 Powerful Habits to Wire Your Mind For Success, Become Truly Happy, and Achieve Financial Freedom* by Stellan Moreira

*Rich AF: The Winning Money Mindset That Will Change Your Life* by Vivian Tu

*Hard Asks Made Easy: How to Get Exactly What You Want* by Laura Fredricks

Rule Your Authordom: *The Step-by-Step Plan to Take Control of Your Writing Career, Work Less, and Earn 6 Figures* by Kel Carpenter

## Shock & awe

If you've got an attention-grabbing title that makes readers do a double-take, you're employing the Shock and Awe titling strategy.

Some terrific examples of this include:

*Building a Second Brain: A Proven Method to Organize Your Digital Life and Unlock Your Creative Potential* by Tiago Forte

*How to Make Your Man Behave in 21 Days or Less Using the Secrets of Professional Dog Trainers* by Karen Salmansohn

*The Subtle Art of Not Giving a F*ck: A Counterintuitive Approach to Living a Good Life* by Mark Manson

*Atomic Habits: An Easy & Proven Way to Build Good Habits & Break Bad Ones* by James Clear

## Make a big promise

State your promise to the reader right on the cover, and tell them exactly what they will gain from reading your book.

Examples include:

*Get Rich, Lucky Bitch* by Denise Dunfield-Thomas
*I Can Make You Thin* by Paul McKenna

*Get Out of Your Head: Stopping the Spiral of Toxic Thoughts* by Jennie Allen

*Manifest Your HEA* by Heather Hildenbrand

## The command

This title style tells the reader what to do. For example:

*Buy Back Your Time: Get Unstuck, Reclaim Your Freedom, and Build Your Empire* by Dan Martell

*Stop Procrastinating: A Simple Guide to Hacking Laziness, Building Self Discipline, and Overcoming Procrastination* by Nils Salzgeber

*Get Out of Your Head: Stopping the Spiral of Toxic Thoughts* by Jennie Allen

## The "how to"

"How-tos" are an extremely popular titling strategy for self-help because it shows the reader what they will learn by reading your book.

*How to Stay in Love* by James J. Sexton. His subtitle: *A Divorce Lawyer's Guide to Staying Together* is doing double duty

– it includes both a promise (stay together) and clarifies his authority on the topic (he's a divorce lawyer – basically a person who watches people break up all day every day.)

*How to Win Friends and Influence People* by Dale Carnegie

## The list

Lists or "X Steps" books are immensely popular with readers, probably because the title makes clear that the author has a solid plan (with steps!) to help the reader solve their problem or reach their goal.

Examples include:

*The 7 Habits of Highly Effective People: Powerful Lessons in Personal Change* by Stephen R. Covey
*5 Steps to a Winning Year* by Apostle Courtney McLean
*12 Rules for Life: An Antidote to Chaos* by Jordan B. Peterson

## The ticking clock

In much the same way that a 7-step list to accomplish their goals is appealing to a reader, so is a defined timeline for success.

*12 Months to $1 Million: How to Pick a Winning Product, Build a Real Business, and Become a Seven-Figure Entrepreneur* by Ryan Moran

*Write a Self-Help Book in 14 Days: The proven step-by-step plan to easily write your nonfiction book – from the bestselling author coach* by Lisa Daily

As you brainstorm your 20-40 title ideas, try to come up with at least one version of your book's title that fits with each naming strategy: Addressing the Reader Directly, Inspire the Reader, Shock & Awe, The Command, The How-To, The List, and The Ticking Clock.

## The power of your subtitle

Another key element for non-fiction book titles is the subtitle. The subtitle can further explain your promise to the reader, or clarify your "reason why" – why is your book the best book on the subject?

As I discussed earlier, the title and subtitle work together to grab the reader's attention (title), and tell them why they need your book to solve their problem. (subtitle). Make your best argument -- See #9 in your CWP.

**BESTSELLER ACADEMY
EXTRA CREDIT**

> **Once you've brainstormed 20-40 title ideas, try writing a subtitle for each. Some subtitles will work for multiple titles, but the exercise of writing subtitles for each of your potential titles is that it can often spur more great title ideas by forcing you to dig a little deeper.**

The title and subtitle of this book are: ***Write a Self-Help Book in 14 Days****: The proven, step-by-step plan to easily write your nonfiction book — from the bestselling author coach*

There's a lot to unpack here.

First, the title, ***Write a Self-Help Book in 14 Days,*** clearly communicates the promise to the reader – read this book and you can write a self-help book in two weeks.

The subtitle takes that a step further. *The proven, step-by-step plan to easily write your nonfiction book — from the bestselling author coach* communicates 1) that the plan to help you write your book in 14 days is **easy to follow** and **proven,** 2) that the book is written by someone with authority, the **bestselling author coach**.

I tend to err on the side of long and useful subtitles. Sure, they can be a bit unwieldy to spit out when you're appearing on TV or a podcast, but they also allow you to clarify your benefit, expertise, or audience – not to mention potentially including some long-tail keywords into your book title for SEO purposes

Here are some key elements to consider in order to make your self-help book title and subtitle memorable:

**Benefits & Solutions:** The most memorable self-help titles often suggest the benefits or solutions readers can gain from the book. If your book offers a solution to a problem, consider at least hinting at it in the title.

**Specificity:** Specific details or numbers in the title can capture the reader's attention and make the content seem more valuable. For example, "7 Steps to Financial Freedom" is more compelling than a vague title like "Financial Freedom."

**Evocative Language:** Use words that evoke emotions, curiosity, or a strong response. For example, words like "transformation," "revolutionize," or "uncover" can create a compelling interest.

**Wordplay:** Consider using clever wordplay, alliteration, or metaphors if they align with your book's content and style. A clever play on words can make your title more memorable.

**Unique Angle**: If your nonfiction book approaches a well-known topic from a unique perspective, highlight that in the title. This can set your book apart from others on the same subject. A great example of this is Rich Dad, Poor Dad.

**Target Audience**: Think about your ideal reader and what resonates with them. Your title should appeal to your specific target audience, addressing their needs and interests. Remember, it's all about the reader! Book titles such as 7 Steps to Financial Freedom for Women use this strategy.

**Credibility**: If you have relevant credentials or expertise, consider incorporating that into the title to establish authority. For example, The Neuroscientist's Guide to Productivity or even The Slacker's Guide to Productivity.

**Problem-Solving**: A title that frames your book as a solution to a common problem can be very effective. For example, Solve Your Baby's Sleep Problems.

**Question or Challenge**: A title that poses a question or challenge can engage the reader's curiosity and make them want to learn more. Can You Make a Million in 12 Months? is an example of this approach.

**Conciseness**: Keep the title as concise as possible. A shorter title is often easier to remember and more visually appealing, especially on the cover of a book. I love Decisive by Chip and Dan Heath, which features a Magic 8 Ball on the cover. This one-word title works with the visual and subtitle to clearly communicate the book is about learning to make better decisions. Another one-word winner: Attached: The New Science of Adult Attachment and How It Can Help You Find—and Keep—Love

**Visualization**: A title that paints a mental picture or conjures vivid imagery can be highly memorable. It can also help readers imagine the content of your book. I love this title: Million Dollar Weekend: The Surprisingly Simple Way to Launch a 7-Figure Business in 48 Hours. Can't you just see your kitchen table littered with sticky notes, Red Bulls and

Cheez Doodles after an intense weekend of mapping out and launching your new million-dollar business idea?

**Jargon Free**: Steer clear of industry-specific jargon or technical language in your title, unless your target audience consists of experts who understand and appreciate it. In other words, no tech bro in-jokes for the title, unless your book is written exclusively for tech bros (who will feel like you're speaking to them in their language.) If you're writing an expert guide for a specific cohort, go right ahead. If you're writing a beginner guide for newbies, they won't get the joke or even know what your book is about.

**SEO Considerations**: If your book is going to be sold online (like every other book), consider incorporating keywords or phrases that are relevant to your book's topic to improve its discoverability. Don't make it weird, but if you can swap in a more SEO-friendly word for a synonym without sacrificing your humanity or readability, then go right ahead.

One strategy to consider when looking up potential keywords for your book is a product I love called Publisher Rocket to search out some of the terms that people who are looking for your type of book are actually searching for on Amazon. It's fairly inexpensive (just over $100), and they never charge you to update the software once you purchase. I've been using the same software (with continual free updates) for more than 15 years. Publisher Rocket is a product created by Dave Chesson (aka Kindlepreneur) and I always find his apps, insight, and advice to be incredibly useful when it comes to marketing books.

## Put your promise on the cover

A memorable self-help book title or plan name should both grab readers' attention and accurately represent the content in your book. It's often a delicate balance between creativity and clarity.

It's important to come up with the name of your plan to help your readers accomplish whatever goal they are trying to accomplish by reading your book. This is because coming up with your plan name early, helps you to really create a strong theme throughout the book, which strengthens the concept of your overall plan, as well as making it easier for readers to engage and understand.

Your book title, and plan name should be: clear, and easy to understand, and remember, and clearly communicate the benefit to the reader.

*Write a Self-Help Book in 14 Days*
*The Overthinking in Relationships Fix*
*Think and Grow Rich*
*How to Win Friends and Influence People*
*Emotional Self-Care for Black Women*
*How to Talk to Anyone*

Think about *The 4-Hour Work Week*: you know exactly what you're getting if you follow all the steps in the book. You will go from working 60 hours a week for a boss you hate to working four hours a week with the ability to live some nomad lifestyle and become the tango champion of Brazil or stay home with your kids.

That, my friend, is a crystal clear benefit.

## Culling down your title list

After I have 20 to 40 decent title ideas, I like to narrow it down to the best three, four or five, and then set them aside for the weekend. After my brain has had a bit of a mini-break, I go back and further narrow them down to the strongest title or plan name.

Often, the best option will just jump out at you. If there's no clear winner in your mind, or you'd like to do some basic A/B or A/B/D/C testing, Facebook is an excellent way to test your audience's response to your best options for $30-$40.

Now, some of you are thinking *hey, I don't want to spend $30,* I'm just going to ask my friends and family members which idea they think is best. This is generally not your best strategy.

While your friends and family may be well-meaning, they may or may not be your target audience, and they are operating from different information than a complete stranger would be — i.e., they already know and like you.

Your family and friends may have some interesting insight, and if you trust their opinion, by all means, you should hear them out. But in order to get a more objective handle on which of your plan names or titles is going to be the better performer, your most effective option is to just throw them into the marketplace and see how they do against each other.

Here's what I mean:

1. Set up for Facebook ads to run simultaneously.

2. Do not select the option where Facebook will pick the best-performing ad, you want to give each ad a chance to stand on its own before the Facebook algorithm just kicks in.

3. For each title test, use the same stock photo for each image. Choose a stock photo that represents the general idea of what your book is about, whether that be weight loss, or achieving business goals, or just being a happier person. Use a site like Canva to create two identical "covers" with the same stock photo or style, and **different titles**. Every element must be exactly the same except the titles you are testing.

4. For each ad, choose the exact same audiences to target your ads to. The audience target will be the same target for your book, which you've already determined with the Creative Work Plan.

5. Your call to action (CTA) is what you tell your readers to do. Your button text should read "learn more" for all of your different ad options.

What link should you use? Link to a landing page for your email platform. (Collect the reader's first name and email address, and title it something like "Be the first to get a sneak peek when this book is released!")

Our primary goal here is simply to find which of your 3-4 title or plan options gets the most clicks for the least amount of money, but you will also likely gain some valuable insight, and you may get a head start on building your mailing list.

**BESTSELLER ACADEMY**
**EXTRA CREDIT**
**Title-Testing Bonus Tip: I also like to Facebook test my book covers, and often I'm just looking for the click. It doesn't really matter where the click goes because the information that I'm looking for is whether or not the buyer clicked, not what they did afterwards. That said, if you're having**

**rds. That said, if you're having your potential readers click on something, anyway, you might as well direct them to your mailing list. Your ad can click to a subscribe link with your mailing list, ask people for their sign-up information and tell them that they will be among the first to know when the book is launching. Even with a small scale test, I've added 50 to 100 people to my mailing list without even trying, just by testing titles, plan, names, and covers.**

It's not important to spend a lot of money to do this, but generally speaking, you'll want to spend $10-$15 for each individual test., And you'll want to do that over 3 to 4 days to get the best results according to Facebook.

I want to give you a word of caution if you have done some Facebook title testing and your favorite has come in third or fourth – but even with that, you're considering just choosing your favorite anyway. Before you do, take a quick look at the difference in the cost-per-click (CPC) between your favorite option, and the option that best performed in the title testing. Now multiply the CPC by 1000 for each. The difference between the cost per click represents the difference in time and money that you will have to spend working harder to promote a book with the title or plan name that doesn't perform as well as another option – it's the road not taken, only quantified.

Because we're starting with our Creative Work Plan, you probably already have a really good idea about who your target audience is. That's great, because that is the same demographic you will use in order to test your Facebook ads.

If you're writing a book for women who are college educated, earning over $100,000 a year who are practicing meditation, Facebook will allow you to very specifically reach your target market.

The availability of specific Facebook targets is not always consistent, meaning that sometimes something with a really large fan base is not available as a target, but something extraordinarily specific, like being an expat in Angola, is available. You'll just have to use your imagination and try to get as close to your target as possible.

The other great thing about doing Facebook ads to test the title or your plan name is that you will immediately get a really good idea about the age and gender of the people who are most likely to respond to your ads, and theoretically, your books. This is a really great thing to keep in mind as you not only write the book, but consider how you plan your marketing efforts for the book itself.

> **If you need help with your title, that's exactly what I do every single day for a living – and I absolutely love it.**
>
> Don't hesitate to book a call to chat with me or my

awesome team.

Please visit **https://tidycal.com/lisadaily/book-coaching-intro** to chat.

I offer multiple services and packages to help you accomplish each and every step listed in this book.

## WRITE NOW: Bestseller Book Building Blocks

- **Brainstorm 20-40 Plan Names**

- **Brainstorm 20-40 Book Title Names (if you haven't settled on a plan name yet, or the plan name doesn't quite work for a book title.)** Focus on a succinct title that clearly communicates your promise to the reader.

- **Brainstorm potential subtitles that address your reader's pain points**

- **Choose the best one to go forward with as a "working title" right now.**

- **Optional:** Test your top 2-5 contenders on Facebook to see how they perform in the real world.

# Chapter 5

# Bestseller Academy Blueprint

Here's a quick overview of my **Bestseller Academy Blueprint**:

1. Define the Problem

2. Introduce Your Catchy Plan Name

3. Introduce yourself briefly and explain why you're qualified to help the reader solve their problem

4. Create a Promise to Your Reader

5. Explain the Problem Journey

6. Prepare Your Reader to Act

7. Your Action Plan

8. Troubleshooting Failure/FAQ

9. The Future and Beyond

10. Give Your Contact Info

11. Resources

Now that you're seeing the basic overview, let's dive in a bit deeper so I can explain exactly what each part means.

I've probably already mentioned this about 747 times previously, but if you have not completed your Creative Work Plan, **stop right now** and do that.

**Do not** start writing your book if you don't yet know the answers to the questions in the CWP, because you'll likely get stuck, or just meander through the book with no clear direction, wasting both your time and your reader's.

Those nine questions are the difference between a smooth and easy book writing process, and one that's fraught with wasted time and energy.

Okay, now that you're armed with all the answers from your Creative Work Plan, let's cover all the key sections you'll need to include in your book:

## 1. Define the problem

Define the problem you're trying to solve for the reader, and who you're trying to solve it for. Use your answers from the Creative Work Plan.

Remember, no book is for everyone— the clearer you are on who your reader is, what she wants, and what's stopping her from getting it, the better off you'll both be.

## 2. Explain your catchy plan name

Reiterate and expand on your benefit-driven title or introduce your catchy Action Plan name.

In many cases, your plan name (or method) and your book title will be exactly the same. That's great! It certainly makes things a bit easier.

Remember – if you've got a book title that does double-duty as an Action Plan title, that's the best!

Here's another simple trick – can you just add "Method" or "Plan" to your book title to create your Action Plan name? My amazing client Heather Hildenbrand wrote a phenomenal self-help targeted to romance authors who are having challenges manifesting the life and career they desire. Her brilliant book is entitled *Manifest Your HEA: Get Unstuck and Create Your Happily Ever After*. Her Action Plan name? The HEA Method.

## 3. Introduce yourself briefly and explain why you're qualified to help the reader solve their problem

I don't want you to go into a 7-page recitation of your resume here – you just need a paragraph or so to explain to the reader why you're qualified to solve their problem.

Example: **Why am I qualified to help you write a self-help book?**

I'm a *USA Today* bestselling self-help author and book coach who's helped everyone from first-time authors to 7-figure *USA Today* bestselling authors write a self help book.

## 4. Create a promise to your reader

What will they gain by reading your book? What's the end goal? What will you deliver? Good news, you've already figured this out before you even started writing with the Creative Work Plan. See how that makes things easier?

Woohoo! The work you did with the Creative Work Plan is already paying off.

## 5. Explain the problem journey

How did your reader come to have this problem? What's the history of the problem? Is it the reader's problem? Society's? Something else?

Relate to your reader here — You've been where they are now, and look how awesome your life is now! You've been broke, out of shape, or all alone, crying into a pizza box on a Saturday night. Now, you hold the secrets to the Universe. This is why they should trust you to help you solve their problem.

## 6. Prepare your reader to act

The reader preparation section is where you prepare your reader to change his/her life (ie — what does the reader need to do to prepare for your big plan of action? Where should they be emotionally? What tool(s) do they need to get started? A notebook? A therapist? An online dating membership? Do they need to take an online quiz to figure out which "type" they are? This is the section where you'll let them know everything they need before they get started, in order to be successful with your plan to help them accomplish their goal.

Can you provide something your reader needs to make their progress through your program easier? One tool I provide in this step is a download of the Creative Work Plan. Why? Because a download or fillable worksheet is usually a lot easier for my readers to use than using the exact same information provided in the book format. This is also the same reason that this book has an accompanying workbook.

As always, I want to make it as easy as possible for you to be successful in writing your book. You have something important to contribute to the world – your perspective, your knowledge, your hard-earned life lessons – and I want to simplify everything I can and help you to do that.

Just as you'll want to make it as easy as possible for *your* readers to accomplish their goal in reading *your* book.

## 7. Your Action Plan for the reader

(This is the meat, the takeaway.) This can be structured into steps (think AA), a timeline, phases, types, or any other "small bite" step-by-step process your reader can and will follow to get them from where they are now to where they want to be.

This is also a great place to incorporate at least one of your reader magnets –a free giveaway designed to make your reader's journey go more smoothly, and get them onto your subscriber list so you can start building a relationship with them.

The more connected you are with your readers, the easier it will become for you to understand the struggles and obstacles they're facing as they work to achieve their goals – and create both free resources as well as offer products and services to help them master them.

## 8. Troubleshooting failure

Falling off the wagon, troubleshooting, challenges — this section contains your advice for when the reader faces common problems along their journey. Be sure to acknowledge it's not always easy to change your life! It isn't! (Otherwise we'd all be wealthy, happily alone or blissfully coupled, living our best lives, and in awesome shape -- not to mention having the best sex of our lives, preferably on a mattress stuffed with $1000 bills.)

This section also helps your readers to realize they're not alone in their challenges – other people (including you!) have been where they are now, and come out smiling on the other side.

You may notice that the Google docs template for the Bestseller Academy Blueprint has a section entitled "Parking Lot". (Thanks to my book coaching client LeighAnn for that fantastic name!) The Parking Lot is where you "park" parts of your book as you are writing that you may want to include but don't really have a home for yet somewhere else in the book. As you write, dump tips, advice, and even whole sections of writing into the Parking Lot. Don't worry, we'll use them later!

If, by the time you reach the Troubleshooting Failure/FAQ section, you still haven't figured out where to put those helpful but outlier sections, you can just repurpose that material into an FAQ (Frequently Asked Questions.)

## 9. The future and beyond

End your book on a positive, uplifting note. Tell your reader you have faith in them and you know they can do this!

Of course they can, they've got you guiding them!

## 10. Give your contact info

Tell the reader how to stay connected with you via your website, books, etc. You're helping your readers CHANGE THEIR LIVES!!! You're pals now! You want to know about their story, their progress, and the problems they're having that you didn't anticipate so that you can help to solve them for future readers.

## 11. Resources

This is a handy page (or pages) at the back of the book that includes a list of the free reader magnets you're offering, your website and social media information, as well as a listing of any other resources, such as books or videos, that you may have referenced throughout the book. Items to consider including in your Resources section:

- All the free reader magnets you've offered in the book. These should go up front!

- Your website and social media channels (We'll also include these in the Contact section of the book as well, but we want to make sure the Resources section is basically one-stop shopping.)

- Links/websites for related products you have recommended

- Further reading (this can be your books or others.) This is certainly not a requirement and can be skipped if you have not recommended any other books, etc throughout your book.

It makes writing significantly easier if you just copy and paste resources into the Resource section as you mention them throughout your book. Then, all you'll need to do is format that section by the time you get to writing it – versus having to read through your entire book again in search of something you mentioned in passing but forgot to include.

Okay, now that we have down the basics of the Bestseller Academy Blueprint, we'll be diving into each section in more detail.

Let's do this!

## WRITE NOW: Bestseller Book Building Blocks

- **<u>Download the Bestseller Book Blueprint</u>**, my Google docs chapter outline template. This handy G-doc outline already includes all the sections of the Blueprint to make your writing easier.

**Note:** The Bestseller Book Blueprint also contains a handy section called **Parking Lot** - this is a place for you to "park" any ideas/sections you want to include in the book that you're not quite sure where they belong yet.

## Chapter 6

# Before You Start Writing, Contemplate Reader Magnets

This might seem a bit premature, but I wanted to bring up the idea of a reader magnet with you *before* you start writing your book. (Even though we are also going to talk about it again at various points in the writing process.)

> **If you are unfamiliar, a reader magnet is something useful or valuable that you give away for free in order to attract subscribers to your newsletter or mailing list.**

For example, if you are writing a dating advice book, your reader magnet might be something like an online dating profile checklist – *7 things you must include in your online dating profile to meet better quality dates.*

If you are writing a weight loss book, you might include a reader magnet, such as a PDF of a seven day, healthy meal plan with the shopping list. Or 9 foods that kill belly fat, or even a free video or video series that demonstrates how to do a particular exercise or prepare food in a certain way. Or a nighttime meditation to help readers overcome their midnight snack habit. (I need this!)

According to the Newsletter Ninja, Tammy LaBrecque, the best newsletter magnets are what she calls a "convertible cookie." A convertible cookie is a newsletter magnet that appeals both to your existing newsletter subscribers as a free gift, and also is attractive to prospects who have not yet signed up for your newsletter list.

You may be thinking, "That's okay, Lisa, I'm not even going to have a newsletter list."

*Please hold while I faint and revive myself.*

OK, I'm back.

Do you need a mailing list? YES, YES YOU DO.

**You absolutely need a subscriber mailing list if you are going to be a successful author, business-owner, or coach.**

> **BESTSELLER ACADEMY EXTRA CREDIT:**
> **An engaged and active subscriber list is an author's superpower.**

I could write an entire book about this, and perhaps, someday I will. But for just today, let me just say that your email newsletter is going to be the single most effective marketing tool you have in order to not only sell your books, but also to grow your business.

This is why, throughout your self-help book, we will be including two to three newsletter magnets, which are essentially helpful tools and other useful freebies to get those readers off the page and onto your list.

I promise you'll thank me later.

The reason I'm putting this chapter in so early in the process of writing your book is that you will often find opportunities to create newsletter magnets, if you are looking to do so, *while you're writing the book.* That's why I'm advising you to pay attention to this *now*, and we'll circle back to it later to make sure you make the most of this opportunity.

Don't worry about actually creating your newsletter magnets at this stage. As you're writing the book, just keep your mind open to tools you might consider providing to your readers for free.

As I'm writing my manuscripts:

1. I go ahead and refer to the reader magnets/downloadable tools as I'm writing as if they already exist, even if I haven't created them yet. Example: *Ready to get started? Go ahead and download my free Bestseller Academy Blueprint here.*

2. Next, I leave myself a note on the manuscript where I've mentioned the reader magnet, so I remember all the places I'll need to add the link later.
Hint – this will be:

**a) in the text of the book,**

**b) in the takeaways/homework sections of the book, and**

**c) in the Resources section of the book.**

Why so many places? We want to make sure the reader can easily find what they need when they're looking for it. Anything we can do to make our reader's journey to accomplishing their goal easier, faster, or more smoothly – we do it!

3. I also go ahead and copy/paste the description of the reader magnet to the Resources section to serve as a reminder so that I'll remember to create it and add a link before the book is published.

Along the same lines, if your business model includes one-on-one coaching, or a digital course, you can also refer to those *occasionally* throughout the text of your book.

You don't want to hit your readers over the head with a bunch of offers where you're trying to sell them something. The intention behind dropping in these newsletter, magnets, or references to services, such as coaching, is just a no-pressure way to a) help your readers achieve their goals more quickly and easily, and b) alert your reader to some of the services you offer in case they find themselves in need of more help.

Like this:

> **If you need help writing your self-help book, that's exactly what I do every single day for a living.**
>
> Don't hesitate to book a Zoom call to chat with me or my team one-on-one.
>
> Please visit **https://tidycal.com/lisadaily/book-coaching-intro** to

> chat.
> I offer multiple services and packages to help you accomplish each and every step listed in this book.

Obviously, you are an expert in your field. Most of your readers will not be. (Otherwise, why would they need your book?) A number of your readers may need or want more help than your book provides, because they either want your expertise in helping them to avoid costly mistakes they might make on their own, or because it's worth it to them to pay you to accomplish the task more efficiently, faster, or simply with greater piece of mind.

## Keep this in mind

We'll talk more about this further along in the book. For now, I just want you to keep in mind that you'll need one to three newsletter magnets that you can offer your readers for free in order to bring them onto your newsletter subscriber list. We're not going to brainstorm about this now, because many of these ideas will bubble up naturally, as you are writing the chapters in the plan section of your book.

For example, if like my client, Renee Rose, author of *Write to Riches,* or my other client, Heather Hildenbrand, author of *Manifest Your HEA*, you are teaching readers to tap into the abundance of the Universe and remove any money blocks that might be standing in their way, you might recommend in the text of the book that your reader try techniques such as journaling, tapping, or meditation.

Offering your reader a free meditation download as part of this chapter provides them with additional and enhanced information that will help them to achieve their goals, and make their path easier.

You want to offer something:

- Useful to their journey or solving their problem,
- That makes executing your plan easier, or is
- Inspiring or fun

It will also land them on your mailing list, where you can provide additional resources to help them accomplish their goals, build a rapport and a relationship with them, give them information about your other services, and more.

Some potential options for reader magnets in your book include but are not limited to:

- A free downloadable report, checklist, white paper,

workbook, or plan.

- An online quiz or assessment

- An exclusive video download

- An exclusive podcast or audio download (such as a meditation audio recording)

Your magnet should be something that is instantly downloadable or available – that way it won't cost you anything other than your time to initially set it up. But it will be working for years to help your readers and clients to achieve their goals faster and easier – which will in turn build your newsletter subscriber list and your business.

That's all I have to say about this topic for now. I just wanted to introduce the idea to you, so that you could be thinking of potential reader magnets to offer your readers, as you are writing each chapter in the plan section of your book.

It is possible that you have already created one or more reader magnets that are a good fit for your book and your target audience. Fantastic! **As you are writing, keep an eye out for a natural place to include them where they will be of benefit to your reader.**

Some of my favorite self-help reader magnet examples include:

- Renee Rose's weekly abundance graphics I can put on my own social media or print out and put in my planner

- Free "starter" media list in *Become a Famous Self-Help Author*

- Cheat sheets or fillable Excel documents

- A discount code for a class, coaching session, or product connected with your book topic. For example, you can use the promo code BESTSELLER50 to get $50 off my Bestseller Academy "Write a Self-Help Book in 30 days" course. (See the Resources chapter at the end of this book for details.)

## WRITE NOW: Bestseller Book Building Blocks

In your workbook (or on your phone, or in your manuscript) jot down any potential ideas you have for your reader magnets right now, and be sure to save ideas as you are writing so you can choose the best 1-3 to implement by the time you finish the book.

Do you have any great reader magnet ideas? What are they?

# Chapter 7

# How to Write Your First Chapters

Ooh! We're getting to the good part!

Now, before you just launch right into your life-changing plan for the reader, you'll need to check in with them to make sure they have everything they need to follow your plan of action.

## What to cover before you get to your Action Plan

The two chapters before the Action Plan are where you prepare your reader and teach them how to change their life.

These early chapters are all about telling your reader what exactly they need to do to *prepare* for your big plan of action.

Where should they be emotionally? What tool(s) if any, do they need to get started? A download? A notebook? A therapist? Membership in a public or private Facebook group? An open mind?

Unless your answer to this section is extremely long, you can generally advise your readers what they'll need:

- Either Chapter 2 (before you outline the actual plan) in just a few lines or a paragraph at the most

- Or at the very beginning of the chapter where you lay out your Action Plan for the reader.

Both are great places to also let readers know that you're pulling for them and you're confident that they can accomplish their goal.

Your Action Plan is the heart of your plan – it's the process by which you are fulfilling your promise to the reader. You'll want to structure your Action Plan into manageable "small bite" steps such as a timeline, phases, by day/week, or any other step-by-step process your reader can and will follow.

My Bestseller Academy Blueprint is broken down into small steps. Because the title of the book, *Write a Self-Help Book in 14 Days* includes a time component, I could also effectively break down the tasks by day if I wanted to. (Note, I've included a 14-day schedule breakdown earlier in the book, but opted out of structuring my book by days, rather than just chronologically, because I don't want to pressure or dissuade anyone who doesn't have a big chunk of time over two weeks to write a book.)

Break down the tasks or goals that must be accomplished in your Action Plan for the reader into small enough chunks so that the reader doesn't get overwhelmed or lost as they work through completing your plan.

You want to strike a balance between small accomplishments that can be achieved in an hour or less and bigger tasks that may take a few days to complete. If a single step takes more than a few days to complete, you'll need to try to break it down into smaller tasks or steps.

## The Bestseller Academy Blueprint is not a chapter guide

The Blueprint has 11 sections, but each one does not represent an individual chapter. They represent the key elements that must be included.

Here's a quick overview:

1. Define the Problem

2. Introduce Your Catchy Plan Name

3. Introduce yourself briefly and explain why you're qualified to help the reader solve their problem

4. Create a Promise to Your Reader

5. Explain the Problem Journey

6. Prepare Your Reader to Act

7. Your Action Plan

8. Troubleshooting Failure

9. The Future and Beyond

10. Give Your Contact Info

11. Resources

## What goes in Chapter 1?

We generally include #1-3 from the Bestseller Academy Blueprint in the first chapter so we can immediately orient the reader and let them know that they've come to the right place. How do we do that? By telling them right away in Chapter one. Your first chapter should include:

- Open with a hook - this can be a memorable anecdote, a shocking statistic, a common misconception, a question, or a surprising statistic related to your reader's problem and your promise.

- Who the book is for, and address your reader's pain points,

- The problem it is designed to fix,

- Why you are qualified to fix it,

- Introduction of the plan with the catchy name that will solve their problem,

- And finally, make a promise (or several) to the reader about how you will help them solve their problem by the end of the book.


All of these are things you've conveniently figured out using the Creative Work Plan *before* you ever started writing, which (taadaa!) will make it incredibly easy to write your first chapter.

If you're unfamiliar with the concept of a hook, it's simply a short, memorable opening to your book. It can be as short as a word or sentence, or as long as a few paragraphs. Some great examples of hooks include:

*"I sat down on Monday to check my email... I never quite know what I'm going to open, but on this particular Monday I opened a note from a fellow author...*

*You're changing lives, I hope you know that. At least, you're changing mine."*

*–The Bestselling Author Next Door*, Skye Warren

This passage has been abridged slightly for space, but the hook is crystal clear – and I need to know RIGHT NOW exactly what Skye is doing to or for this author. Don't you?

*"Do you ever wonder how some writers seem to crank out story after story, article after article, book after book? Or why it is that so many people dream of writing a novel but so few ever do? Whether you are a blogger, a researcher, or an aspiring novelist, how would your life change if you could consistently produce your best writing?"*

– *The 12 Week Year for Writers*, A. Trevor Thrall

*"My hands were sweating again.*

*Staring down at the floor to avoid the blinding ceiling lights, I was supposedly one of the best in the world but it just didn't register. My partner Alicia shifted from foot to foot as we stood in line with nine other couples, all chosen from over 1,000 competitors from 29 countries and four continents. It was the last day of the Tango World Championship semifinals, and this was our final run in front of the judges, television cameras, and cheering crowds. The other couples had an average of 15 years together. For us, it was the culmination of 5 months of nonstop 6-hour practices, and finally it was showtime."*

–*The 4-Hour Workweek*, Timothy Ferriss

And finally, one of my very favorite hooks in a self-help book comes from *Make Time: How to Focus on What Matters Every Day* by Jake Knapp and John Zeratsky.

It includes minimal text, and some hand-drawn illustrations. I love it and it's hooky as can be.

I talk like that! My calendar looks like that! And suddenly, I'm assured that these fine gentlemen Jake and John understand my pain and have figured out a way to solve it. (They have actually, I highly recommend *Make Time*.)

In addition to (or as part of) a great hook, you'll want to make sure you address some of your reader's pain points in your first chapter.

This serves two purposes. First, it allows the reader to see themselves in your book right away. Second, if you show your reader that you understand what is causing them pain or keeping them stuck, you're already 90% of the way there to showing them that you (and your book) are the solution to solve their pain and help them achieve their goals.

Finally, you'll want to round out the chapter with your promise/promises to the reader. (Yes, the same ones you figured out in your Creative Work Plan.

Feel free to use bullet points, and start the sentence with:

**By the time you finish this book, you will learn:**

- **This!**

- **This!**

- **This other thing!**

- **And THIS incredible thing!**

## What's in Chapter 2?

In your second chapter, you'll want to cover #4 and #5 from the Blueprint including:

- The Problem Journey and

- Reader Preparation

In other words, how did your reader come to have the problem and what do they need to have on hand (or downloaded) in order to execute the advice you're giving them?

Remember back in Chapter 2? I shared my own frustrating process with trying to figure out how to write a self-help book, and explained that in order to get started with the Bestseller Academy Blueprint all you need is:

1. The download of my Creative Work Plan

2. A word processing program like Google docs or Word

3. A commitment to block off time in your calendar to actually get your writing done, and

4. Bonus– An email list platform you can use to communicate with your readers and deliver your email magnets.

## Why do we front-load the book with all these goodies?

The reason we put all those important items up front is so that your reader can begin executing your plan as quickly as possible – right now while they're all fired up and excited to change their life and accomplish their goal.

That momentum fuels their success and we want to get them up to speed as quickly as we possibly can.

> **BESTSELLER ACADEMY**
> **EXTRA CREDIT**
> **It's my goal to remove every barrier, difficulty, pain point, or obstacle I possibly can to help you to achieve your goal of writing a self-help book.**

It's *your* job to remove as many barriers, difficulties, pain points, or obstacles within your book and reader magnets for *your* reader.

*How can you make things easier for your reader?* Always, always keep them in mind, and do whatever you can to smooth their path.

You'll want to make sure you keep all the pain points you came up with in the Creative Work Plan in mind throughout writing the book – so you can address them and remove the barriers for your readers at every possible opportunity.

I want to do everything in my power to help you succeed in writing your book. Just as you will want to do everything in your power to help your readers succeed at what you're teaching them.

## A word on formatting

As you write your self-help book, there are a few things you'll need to know:

## 1. It doesn't really matter what writing platform you use.

You can use Google docs, Word, Butterdocs, Scrivener, Atticus, or any one of dozens of writing programs. They all work pretty much the same. I have used most of them on a wide variety of projects, and find Google Docs is pretty easy to work with, especially for my coaching clients because it's free and collaboration is easy.

For years, I wrote my books using Microsoft Word, which worked just fine. I eventually switched from Word to G-docs because Microsoft switched from a "software you paid once for" model to a subscription model, and I could not bring myself to pay every month for a product that had not significantly changed or improved in 20 years.

That said, money wasn't the only factor in my decision-making process – I also used Scrivener for several books, and was always frustrated by the "compiling" process which I could never seem to remember due to the months between completed books.

Now I use G-docs to write and collaborate with my book coaching students.

## 2. Use lots (and lots) of subtitles in your chapters.

Self-help readers are often information seekers who do not read for fun. This is why it's incredibly important to deliver your message to them in a way that makes it easily digestible.As you finish writing each chapter, review it by reading only the subtitles. Can you get the general gist of the chapter without reading the text? Great! If not, add some more subtitles to break things up, and highlight the main points in your text

## 3. Use lots of bullet points, lists, pull quotes, graphics, and text boxes to break up the text.

Break up long sections of text to keep readers' attention and interest.

## 4. Include takeaways of important points "Key Points" and/or "Homework" at the end of your chapters.

Takeaways summarize the key content in the chapter to make it easier to remember. "Homework" is useful if you are trying to teach someone to do something and you want them to actively follow along.

For example, most chapters in this book have homework assignments. Why? I'm teaching you to write a self-help book, and it will be a lot easier for you to be successful in that endeavor if you write the book step-by-step as I explain the process to you (rather than trying to remember every single thing I said, and then somehow turn all that newly-acquired knowledge into a book without missing anything, skipping steps, or wasting time.) It also helps you to highlight the information that you feel is most important for your reader.

Homework also helps your readers to build confidence in the new skills they're learning, and allows them to experience those highly motivating "wins" as they work towards accomplishing their bigger goal. Yay you!

## 5. Include your reader magnets

- Within the text as you are describing their purpose or necessity to the reader

- At the end of the chapter, either in homework or key takeaways

- At the end of the book in the resources section.

Is all that repetition really necessary? Yes. Often your reader will want the free tool you're providing to them, but may forget exactly where they saw it. Once again, you always want to make it as easy on your reader as possible.

## 6. Write in 2nd person (i.e., "You" "we")

Talk to your reader as though you're having a conversation with just one person. "You may be wondering," feels far more personal and relevant to the human being reading your book than "Some people may wonder" which feels much more detached. A self-help book should be a conversation between the author and the reader. Having a rough time actually putting that into action? Imagine you're speaking directly to your reader avatar – that real or imaginary person who is the ideal reader of your book.

## 7. Don't "because I said so" your reader

One challenge I sometimes see with my book coaching clients is that they'll sometimes tell their reader to do something, without telling them why. It's really important to let the reader know why you're telling them to do a specific action, especially if it's:

- Something that is a departure from common wisdom (Everyone else says "go left" and you say "go right")

- Important for your reader to accomplish as they are completing your Action Plan

- Something you want them to actually *do* — we're far more likely to take action if we actually know why it matters

Nobody really appreciates "do it because I said so", and worse, they rarely learn from it. Tell your readers *why* you're telling them to do what you're telling them to do.

## 8. Include case studies, stories, and real-life examples throughout your chapters

Human beings learn through storytelling. Do you have case studies or examples you can use in your book to illustrate some of the challenges, pain points and successes your readers may have? Let's put them in!

## 9. Make your plan logical and linear

Clearly communicate what your reader needs to learn, know, understand, and execute *in order* to be successful in solving their problem or challenge. Focus on what the reader should do chronologically (first, next, next, then, finally) so that it's easy for them to not only follow along, but also execute your plan in the most efficient way possible.

## 10. Cite your sources

If your plan or idea came entirely from your own brain, well, that's great. But oftentimes, we read a book or acquire some of the information that leads to our expertise in a certain area from someone else. If you are teaching your reader a lesson that references someone else's work, be sure to cite your source. It doesn't need to be complicated, it can be as simple as this:

In *Write to Riches*, my book coaching client Renee Rose discusses an energy-clearing resource she's used: "[*The Sedona Method*] is a book by Hale Dwoskin that's available in audio format. It presents a really clear, simple five-step method to let go of things. I have a lot of travel anxiety, and I read this book right before a trip once and used the methods on my drive to the airport. By the time I arrived, I was practically floating in total ease and relaxation!"

**BESTSELLER ACADEMY**
**EXTRA CREDIT**

**It's always helpful to include any books you've quoted, or think might be useful to your reader in your "Resources" chapter at the end of your book. Save yourself a headache by copy-pasting recommended and cited books (and other resources you mention, such as YouTube videos) into the Resources chapter as you go. Then, all you need to do when you write that section is formatting and proofreading!**

## WRITE NOW. Bestseller Book Building Blocks:

**Write Chapters 1 & 2 of your book.** Use your answers from the Creative Work Plan (CWP) and use the Bestseller Academy Blueprint.

**Chapter One should include:**
- A hook - something to grab the reader right away and keep them reading

- Who the book is for, addressing your reader's pain points

- The problem your book is designed to fix,

- Why you are qualified to fix the reader's problem (your education, your experience, etc),

- Introducing your plan with the catchy name to teach them to solve their problem step-by-step,

- And finally, make a promise (or several) to the reader about how you will solve the problem by the end of the book.

**Chapter Two should include:**
- This chapter includes the reader's problem journey. *How did they come to have the problem they're reading your book to solve?* and,

- Reader preparation. What does your reader need to do or have right now in order to start executing your plan?

## Chapter 8

# The Meat! Your Action Plan for the Reader

How are you feeling about your first two chapters? Pretty good, right?

Once you have them completed, go back and review to make sure that each chapter you've written includes all the mandatories outlined in the previous chapter.

Great job!

**Your Action Plan**

Next we're going to start writing the "Action Plan" section of your book. You can expect this section to span multiple chapters in your book.

It is, in fact, the majority of the "meat" your book, because this is where you actually show your readers how to get from point A, where they are now (switching every few minutes between banging their head against a wall and weeping into a vat of cookie dough) to point B, where they want to be (your promise fulfilled, with their goal accomplished or firmly in reach.)

You've probably already done this next step when completing the Creative Work Plan. But if you haven't, take a few minutes right now to write down all the steps your reader will need to take to accomplish their goal. Generally, you'll want to do this in chronological (time) order because that's the easiest way for your reader to learn.

Start by writing a numbered list with a single line of explanation for each step, like this:

Your Action Plan
1.
2.
3.
4.

5.
6.
7.
8.
9.
10...

**EXAMPLE: Here's a quick overview of the Bestseller Academy Blueprint Action Plan:**

1. Define the Problem
2. Introduce Your Catchy Plan Name
3. Introduce yourself briefly and explain why you're qualified to help the reader solve their problem
4. Create a Promise to Your Reader
5. Explain the Problem Journey
6. Prepare Your Reader to Act
7. Your Action Plan
8. Troubleshooting Failure
9. The Future and Beyond
10. Give Your Contact Info
11. Resources

Now, you'll probably notice that if you compared my Action Plan against my table of contents, that they wouldn't necessarily line up. Why?

First of all, some of the mandatories in my Action Plan (such as number 9, Give Your Contact Info) do not actually require a whole chapter to themselves. You just need to make sure you include it in your self-help book in the same general area, near the end of the book. Second, there are several extra chapters in my book, such as those on creating a workbook or incorporating reader magnets that are super-helpful to *my* readers (aka you!) but that wouldn't be useful to your readers at all.

The Action Plan is just the A to B to C part of your book that takes your reader, step-by-step to accomplishing their goal.

Let's take a look at how this might work for a different type of self-help book.

**EXAMPLE: Here's an Action Plan for a book that shows you how to make pizza from scratch at home:**

1. Gather necessary ingredients and supplies
2. Prepare the Dough
3. Add the Sauce and Toppings
4. Bake the Pizza
5. Optional Finishing Touches
6. Pizza Recipes to Try

Your Action Plan may be more or fewer steps than the one listed above. The sweet spot is somewhere in the neighborhood of 4 - 15 steps.

All of the sections in my Blueprint plan can be completed in less than a day, with the exception of the Action Plan. Because we want to keep our reader moving forward through our process, we're going to break up any bigger steps that take more than a few days into smaller chunks if at all possible.

Don't worry if you think and think on it and just can't seem to figure out a way to break down a lengthier step. It's really not the end of the world if it will take the reader a week or a few weeks to accomplish a particular step of your plan. That said, those longer steps should be *very* limited in number and should always follow at least 1-2 easier, quicker wins to keep the reader motivated and feeling like they're making progress.

## Work *with* human nature, not against it

The exception to the *Probably nobody will die if you have a step that takes more than a couple of days* rule: A two-week step should absolutely, positively *never* be the first step in your Action Plan.

Why? It's hard to find the motivation to change our lives, even when we want to. Part of effective instructional design (teaching people how to learn something new in the most effective way possible) is giving students early successes so they stay focused and motivated.

How could I break down my longest step, number 6, Your Action Plan, into smaller, more manageable chunks for you?

**BESTSELLER ACADEMY
EXTRA CREDIT
When breaking down bigger steps, I think about how I might be able to separate the "thinking part" of the step from the actual execution, or "doing part".**

The Action Plan is the main section of your book, so it's crucial we get it right. Because it's really important to the success of the reader, I'm first asking you to list the steps of your plan in order, so you can make certain you're providing your reader with everything they need to be successful.

Then, further break down any big steps that might slow the reader's progress.

So, in the case of the **Bestseller Academy Blueprint**, aka step 6, Your Action Plan becomes:

6(a) Make a list of the steps in your Action Plan,

6(b) Break down any steps that will take more than a few days into smaller steps.

6(c) Review the list of steps and see if it makes sense to batch several steps together into chapters, or whether each step requires its own chapter.

6(d) Write the individual Action Plan chapters

Smaller "chunks" feel more manageable for your reader. And that's good, because we don't just want the reader to buy your book. We want them to:

- Be successful in accomplishing the goal that was the reason for them buying your book in the first place

- Write rave reviews on Amazon and tell all their friends that you and your book are the reason they were able to finally achieve their goal

- Subscribe to your newsletter and hire you as a coach, enroll in your courses, or become a member of your Mastermind group because they know they can trust you to help them accomplish their goals.

## WRITE NOW. Bestseller Book Building Blocks:

1. **Write a numbered list with a single line of explanation for each step in your Action Plan.** What steps does your reader need to take to get them from where they are now to where they want to be?

   Will any of the steps require more than a few days to accomplish? Is it possible to break down those longer steps even further?

2. **Review the list of steps you've just written, and make a decision.** Does it make sense to batch several steps together into chapters? Or will it be more effective to give each step its own chapter? Will some steps require multiple chapters? If you are in doubt here, then opt to make each step its own chapter. You can always combine two or three short related chapters later.

# Chapter 9

# Anatomy of an Action Plan Chapter

Okay, now you've broken down your Action Plan into steps, and if necessary, quicker sub-steps, it's time to write the Action Plan chapters of your book.

**Action Plan chapters should include:**

1. **A clear step or lesson**, with direct instructions on what the reader must do next.

2. **At least one story, example, or case study** to illustrate a problem and/or the solution.

3. **Any additional tips**, lessons learned, or resources to help your reader accomplish that step of the Action Plan more efficiently or effectively.

4. **Key takeaways or homework for each step**, formatted in a text box at the end of each chapter. (Or both) This helps to ensure that your reader is taking action and actually working through your plan, rather than just passively reading about it. Why is this important? Many self-help readers will essentially try to succeed through osmosis — meaning they read your book but don't follow the plan. Giving homework at the end of each Action Plan chapter helps readers to understand what's important, causes them to take action, and gives them some momentum when it comes to actually doing the steps you've outlined in your book. Homework helps your reader accomplish their goal.

5. **Headings, bullet points, numbered lists, pull quotes, and visuals** to break up text and make it easy for readers to navigate and engage with your material.

6. At least one of your Action Plan chapters should include **a reader magnet** such as a PDF, audio download, video, mini-course, or anything else you can provide as a download to help your reader work through your plan more quickly or easily.

If you're struggling with exactly how to structure your Action Plan, start first by trying to figure out how your advice might be lumped into 3 - 5 sections

## Teach your Action Plan chronologically

90% of the time, it is best to teach your Action Plan chronologically, meaning, teach your reader the steps to accomplish their goal in the order they should do them.

Think of how you'd typically describe to someone how to do something:
First, do this.
Next, do this.
Then, do this.
Finally, do this.

That's all you need to know to structure your Action Plan – just tell your reader exactly what to do, step-by-step, and the exact order in which to do it. It's that simple!

## Tips for success

Be sure to:
- Follow the Bestseller Academy Blueprint,

- Use clear and informative chapter names,

- Utilize frequent, skimmable subtitles, and

- Include key takeaways and/or homework at the end of each chapter.

## Parking lot

If you're like most of my book coaching clients, you probably started your self-help book project with a collection of random ideas and tips that you wanted to share. As you work through the Creative Work Plan to create your Action Plan and get your advice organized in a way that makes it logical and actionable for your reader, you may find you have some good stuff that you're not quite sure where it fits. No problem! Simply drop these ideas/sections into the Parking Lot section of the Blueprint. Once you've completed your Action Plan chapters, go back to see which of those Parking Lot tips/sections can be effectively incorporated into an existing chapter in your Action Plan, or add them to your Troubleshooting chapter as an FAQ.

For now, anything you want to say that doesn't belong somewhere else goes in the FAQ.

> **BESTSELLER ACADEMY**
> **EXTRA CREDIT**
> **When starting with a big pile of stuff, it's generally most effective to see if you can group your advice into smaller subgroups, either by topic or chronologically.**

# Big Pile of Stuff Method (aka Bucket Method)

One of my clients, Skye Warren, a major seven-figure romance author, had been sending out newsletters containing publishing advice for several years to her subscriber list of authors looking to level up their own author careers. Skye is one brilliant marketer, and when we first started working together on her book, she forwarded about a hundred emails with some incredible advice that she wanted to build into a self-help book. You may be starting with something similar.

Skye is truly unique in that she earns millions from her books, despite the fact that she has a chronic medical condition that prevents her from working more than a few hours a day. Working three hours a day and still raking in seven figures from your books is the dream for most authors, and so we knew Skye's self-help book, *The Bestselling Author Next Door* was going to be a massive hit.

Because she organizes her own writing and book marketing efforts by quarter, focusing one month each quarter on either *writing*, *marketing*, or promoting her *backlist*, our first step was to organize the emails by subject and try to see which pieces of her advice fit into one of those three buckets.

Another reason this strategy was successful was because Skye's quarterly system is unique among authors, most of whom are relying on the *try to do everything you possibly can, all the time, until you burn out* strategy.

Once we did that, we were able to further break down each of the three sections (writing/marketing/backlist) of the Action Plan into smaller steps within each section. The marketing section, for example, included specifics on how to structure a romance series, what to include in your book's backmatter, and how to run Facebook ads, among other things. Because Skye organized her own author business efforts in a 3-month rotation, it was natural to structure her book in a way that laid out that same strategy for her readers, allowing them to easily mimic her methods (and hopefully her success!)

And even though we broke Skye's Action Plan into her yearly quarters, within each section (writing, marketing, and backlist) her advice within the sections was primarily structured chronologically.

## Buffet Style

Another approach to structuring your Action Plan is what I like to call Buffet Style, meaning the reader can basically pick and choose what is important to them, without having to go through the entire book.

A key advantage of structuring the book into Buffet Style sections is that it allows readers to jump to the particular section they're most interested in or working through at the moment.

The Action Plan for my client Lee Savino, a 7-figure romance and self-help author of *Adventures With the Universe,* was essentially a series of abundance manifestation "games" with the Universe that could be played in any order, depending on what was most appealing to the reader.

This strategy can also be effective if your book is primarily problem-solving in specific buckets. For example, let's say you were writing a book about how to get your baby to sleep through the night. (These books are perennial bestsellers because sleep-deprived parents are desperate and will read or do *anything* for a little relief. *Make a beef jerky ritual sacrifice at 2 am while howling at the moon? Done.*)

You might structure this type of book either chronologically (do this first, do this next) – no matter where the non-sleeping baby is starting in his or her ability to sleep through the night. It's basically the baby equivalent of unplugging your internet router and plugging it back in again – a reset.

In this case, your Action Plan might look something like this:

1. Set up a sleep diary

2. Create a separate sleep space for baby

3. Simplify baby's diet

4. Create a bedtime routine

5. Using cribs, mobiles, weighted sleepers and other tools

6. Put baby on a sleep/wake/play/eat/sleep schedule

7. Adjust schedule as needed

8. Brag to other parent friends once you're getting 8 hours of shuteye a night.

Or, you might approach the issue Buffet Style, with different solutions for different issues under the same "How to get your baby to sleep" umbrella.

In this case, your Action Plan might look something like this:

1. What to do if your baby wakes up more than twice per night for feedings

2. What to do if your baby wakes up every time you put him down

3. What to do if your baby sleeps well in a bassinet or swing, but won't sleep in a crib

4. What to do if your baby refuses to go to sleep at a reasonable hour

5. What to do if your baby won't go back to sleep after a midnight feeding...

You get the picture.

Same problem, probably the exact same information, but entirely different approaches.

## Gryffindor Style

The Gryffindor Style (named for Harry Potter's house at Hogwarts because that was the very first thing that popped into my head) is when you structure your Action Plan chapters to address specific types or groups.

Generally when using this type of approach, you'll include a quiz or assessment tool your readers can use to figure out which *type* they are.

**REMEMBER: If you're planning on utilizing this type of tool, you'll need to include it in your Reader Preparation section.**

You have two options here:

1. Either include the quiz or assessment in the Reader Preparation section along with self-scoring instructions, or

2. You can send your reader to a third-party site (like Paperform, Typeform, Buzzfeed, or Survey Monkey) to take the quiz and figure out which "type" they are.

One of my awesome book coaching clients, Kel Carpenter included a quiz in her book, *Rule Your Authordom,* to help her readers decide whether they should publish wide or in Kindle Unlimited.

Whichever you choose, the quiz or assessment **must be free**. It is unfair and bad business (not to mention bad Karma) to expect your readers to pay for the information necessary to use the book they've *already* paid their hard-earned money to buy.

My recommendation? Use a third-party site for your quiz, or host it on your own website. That way, you can collect the emails from all your readers who take the test, build your subscriber list, and be able to contact them in the future with other advice, products, and services you may offer to help them achieve their goals.

An Action Plan using Gryffindor Style for *Hogwarts Guide to Love: Use your Hogwarts house to find your perfect match* might look like this:

1. Gryffindor

2. Hufflepuff

3. Ravenclaw

4. Slytherin

Are you an astrologist writing a self-help book about how to find love or succeed in business based on your horoscope? Your Gryffindor Style Action Plan would most likely look like this:

1. Capricorn

2. Aquarius

3. Pisces

4. Aries

5. Taurus

6. Gemini

7. Cancer

8. Leo

9. Virgo

10. Libra

11. Scorpio

12. Sagittarius

The insanely smart, bestselling author coach Becca Syme created a plan for authors to level up their careers by leaning into the Archetypes she's identified. Her Action Plan might look something like this:

1. Tundra

2. Evergreen

3. Island

4. Trailblazer

5. Phoenix

The most important thing to remember about using the Gryffindor Style is that you'll need to provide your "sorting hat" assessment early in the book, in your Reader Preparation section. You should know that readers *love* quizzes — and a "sorting hat" quiz is a spectacular reader magnet.

## Titling your Action Plan chapters

Coming up with titles for each of your Action Plan chapters doesn't have to be as complicated as brainstorming your Book Title and/or Action Plan name. It's generally my preference to keep things short and simple, and basically describe what each step entails.

Do I enjoy a little alliteration, wit, and wordplay? Absolutely. If you do too, drag out that rapier wit of yours and go ahead and brainstorm away. That said, when writing self-help, it's super important to be crystal clear with your reader about what they need to do now, and what they'll be doing next. In other words, if you have to pick, **choose clarity over creativity**.

If you can do both at the same time, by all means, do.

### Subtitles, glorious subtitles

I mentioned this previously in an earlier chapter, but it bears repeating. Subtitles are sooooo important when it comes to making your self-help book effective. Why? A lot of self-help readers don't read for enjoyment, they read for knowledge. Subtitles help them stay on track, and provide a sort of outline for those readers who tend to skim.

## Give your tips a consistent name based on your plan name

Periodically throughout your book, it can be useful to create bolded tips to highlight critical information. Be sure to give your tips a consistent name, based on your title or plan name.

My plan name is The Bestseller Academy Blueprint, so I'm using Bestseller Academy Extra Credit for my "don't miss" tips, and put them in a text box for extra emphasis, like this:

> **BESTSELLER ACADEMY EXTRA CREDIT**
> **You can give your homework assignments a consistent and catchy name throughout the book, which will help cue readers to look for them at the end of each chapter. Mine are called "Bestseller Book Building Blocks".**

## WRITE NOW. Bestseller Book Building Blocks:

Write your Action Plan chapters. Remember, each Action Plan chapter should include:

1. A clear step or lesson, with direct instructions on what the reader must do next

2. AT least one story, example or case study to illustrate a problem and/or the solution

3. And additional tips, lessons learned, or resources to help your reader accomplish that step of the Action Plan more efficiently or effectively.

4. Key takeaways or homework, formatted in a text box or graphic pull-out at the end of each chapter.

5. At least one of your Action Plan chapters should include a reader magnet. You can include more if you'd like, and you can place them anywhere in the book where the reader would find them most useful.

# Chapter 10

# Your Final Chapters

You're so close now! We've got a few sections of the Blueprint left to cover before you're finished writing your book. They are:

7. Troubleshooting Failure
8. The Future and Beyond
9. Give Your Contact Info
10. Resources

While technically this might seem like a big job to write two to three more chapters, these final few tend to go pretty quickly. The Troubleshooting Failure chapter will likely be the longest and most challenging to write of the final four sections, but they're all very straightforward and simple – and if you're anything like most of my book coaching clients (smart, good looking , and determined to make a difference) you'll likely knock them out fairly quickly.

Depending on length, I sometimes give the Troubleshooting Failure section its own chapter because it tends to be pretty information-dense, or if it feels right, you can lump it together with The Future and Beyond & Give Your Contact Info.

Finally, I generally give the *Resources* section its own chapter – primarily because I often refer to it throughout the text of the book, and I don't want anybody to get lost when they're trying to find it.

You're almost to the finish line. Let's finish your book!

Here's a breakdown of the last few sections you'll need to include:

## Troubleshooting Failure

I will confess, I love this section. It makes for a fantastic catch-all for anything you wanted to put in the book but didn't find a home for. Plus, it's a great place to address your readers' most common questions.

1. Remember the Parking Lot section of the Blueprint, where you stashed any of your good ideas that didn't have a home yet? Great news! Any topics you wanted to cover but haven't found the right place for can

go in the Troubleshooting/FAQ section. Once you've reached the end of the book, cruise through the parking lot and add any remaining sections into chapters where they fit, or convert them to questions for your FAQ section.

Just make up a question that works with the paragraph or section you'd like to include.

1. Add common questions (and your answers) from your readers or coaching clients to this section.

2. Don't have clients yet? You'll still want to answer some of the most popular questions from people who are searching Google for your particular topic. Not sure about your readers' most common questions? Well, good news for you, Google knows *exactly* what they are.

Just type in your promise or book title into the Google search bar and scroll down a bit. Google will actually tell you what the most common questions are around your topic!

When I typed in *How to write a self-help book* in Google, I got the following commonly asked questions:

> People also ask
> How to write a self-help book for beginners?
> Can anybody write a self-help book?
> What is the format of a self-help book?
> How many pages should a self-help book be?
> Feedback

I'll be sure to address these questions, and any others I can think up, in the Troubleshooting Failure/FAQ section at the end of this book.

Just remember, your Troubleshooting Failure (FAQ) chapter contains your advice for when the reader faces common problems along their journey. Be sure to acknowledge it's not always easy to change your life! – It isn't! Otherwise we'd all be sitting on a beach somewhere with a brilliant and affectionate supermodel rubbing our shoulders while cabana boys bring endless margaritas and an algorithm dumps insane amounts of cash into our very full bank accounts.

There are many ways to structure this part of your book, but I generally find the most straightforward is just an FAQ (Frequently Asked Questions) format. You can group them together by any method that makes sense to you – by topic, chronologically, etc.

One last thing – before you complete the Troubleshooting Failure section of your book, **make sure you have addressed**

**every single pain point you uncovered in the CWP, and every promise you made to your reader in Chapter 1.** If not, either add the information into an existing chapter or include it in this section as an FAQ.

## The Future and Beyond

This section can either be its own chapter or tacked on to the end of the FAQ.

Be sure to end your book on a positive, uplifting note. Tell your reader you have faith in them and you know they can do this!

This section is basically a pep talk on a page. You've given your reader all your best ideas and every tool they need to accomplish their goal. Let them know that you fully believe they can pull it off. And why wouldn't they? They're following your awesome plan!

## Give Your Contact Info

Tell the reader how to stay connected with you via your website, your books, your Substack, etc.

You're helping your readers CHANGE THEIR LIVES!!! Do you know what a big deal that is? It's big. Like, *really* big.

You want to know about their story, their progress, and the problems they're having that you didn't anticipate so that you can solve them for future readers. Some ideas for your readers to keep in contact with you after they finish your book include:

- Facebook groups or your Discord

- Link to subscribe to your newsletter or substack

- Your website, email or phone number depending on how you'd like your readers to contact you

- Your social media

## Resources

The Resources chapter is simply a handy place at the end of the book where your readers can find all the various resources you've referenced throughout the book.

**Always start your Resources section with your reader magnets** – because the section is where your readers are likely to look first when they're searching for them.

You can include anything you like in your resources section, but here are some ideas to start you off:

- Your reader magnets (free downloads to make your reader's journey easier)

- Books or videos you've referenced throughout your book

- Helpful websites and platforms, including yours

- A QR code leading to your download site

- Anything else you'd like to include for your readers!

I continually add to my Resources section as I'm writing the book. Any resources I happen to mention in a chapter I just cut and paste right into the Resources section as well. That way, when I'm nearing the end of writing my book, I can just format what's already there and make sure all the links work. Easy peasy.

## One last thing.

Before you finish writing your book, go back to your first chapter and take a look at your promise to the reader. Did you deliver on everything you said you would? Great! You're ready to move to the next step. If not, be sure to add in any additional information your reader will need (and more specifically, everything you promised) to accomplish their goal.

### DO THIS NOW. Bestseller Book Building Blocks:

**Write these 4 quick sections and rename them for your book:**

- Troubleshooting Failure / FAQ
- The Future and Beyond
- Give Your Contact Info
- Resources

I frequently group these last four sections into 2 chapters, depending on the material – generally FAQ,, Future and Beyond, and my Contact Info go into a single chapter, and I give Resources its own chapter. You can do the same, or structure them a different way that works better for your book – just as long as you include all the information.

# Chapter 11
# Create Your Reader Magnets

Back in Chapter 6, I let you know how important reader magnets can be when it comes to helping your readers be successful in achieving their goals – but also in **building your relationship with your readers, building your business, and frankly, selling your books, coaching, courses, and other products down the line.**

Providing downloadable tools can be a fantastic way for you to add value for your readers, and that should be the key thing you keep in mind as you create your reader magnets.

Ask yourself:

- Is there a tool or cheat sheet I can provide my reader for free to help them accomplish their goal faster?

- Can I provide something my reader can download to

help them jump-start their success?

- What types of "bonuses" would my reader enjoy or appreciate most?

Here's a list of reader magnet ideas to get you started:

1. **Fillable forms or spreadsheets** that readers can download and customize, such as a Google sheet that will calculate your read-through on a romance or mystery series, or a budget tool that helps you to calculate how much you should be saving each week.

2. **Quizzes and Assessments:** A self-assessment questionnaire to help readers evaluate and improve their emotional intelligence, find out where their money blocks are, or self-sort themselves into a particular group or type (think Clifton Strengths, Myers-Briggs, Hogwarts houses, or even horoscopes.)

3. **Self-Reflection Journal:** A printable journal with prompts and exercises for self-reflection and personal growth.

4. **10-Day Challenge**: A 10-day quick start guide with daily activities and prompts to promote mental, emotional, financial, or physical well-being, or to accomplish a specific goal.

5. **Meditation Audio Series**: A series of guided meditation recordings to help readers on areas related to your topic, such as building confidence, tapping for a specific outcome, or mindfulness.

6. **Daily or Weekly Affirmations Printable Cards**: Printable cards or social media posts with empowering affirmations to boost confidence and self-esteem.

7. **Video downloads**: This can be a "look over my shoulder as I do this thing" type video, a meditation, or even a mini-class to teach a helpful, related skill your reader might need.

8. **Mini Goal Setting Workbook or Worksheet:** A workbook with step-by-step instructions and templates for setting and achieving a meaningful, small goal necessary to achieve your reader's bigger goal.

9. **Stress Management Toolkit:** Tools and techniques for managing stress and building resilience while working towards their goal.

10. **Gratitude Journal Prompts**: A list of gratitude journal prompts to inspire readers to cultivate a daily gratitude practice.

11. **Habits Checklist:** Part of learning a new behavior or reaching a new goal is in developing new habits. Offer

your readers a downloadable checklist of daily habits and practices to help them reach their goals.

12. **A Cheat Sheet:** An overview of key principles and exercises from your book they can refer to easily.

13. **A Mini eBook**: A free, short ebook on a related topic useful to your reader.

14. **Training Guide:** A one-page PDF on tips and strategies for developing specific skills or setting healthy boundaries.

## Why offer reader magnets?

- Everybody loves freebies, including your reader.

- Readers appreciate the value of getting something extra for free

- Freebies create reader goodwill

- Helps you to better serve your customers because the

popularity (or lack of) each magnet makes a great roadmap to show you where your readers need the most help, and what tools you can provide they find most useful.

- Allows you to add your readers to your email subscriber list, so that you can easily reach them when you have new advice, tips, tools, coaching, or products to share that might help them to achieve their goals.

- You can also offer your reader magnets on social media to help build a bigger audience for your book and other services. I love it when I can repurpose the awesome content I've already created, don't you?

## How to implement your reader magnets, step by step

As you create your reader magnets, you'll need to do a few things to make the whole thing go.

**1. Create at least one reader magnet right now to include in your book.** Review your own list of ideas from your workbook and the list included in this chapter and choose 1-3 that will best serve your readers. Go ahead and record that meditation, set up that quiz, or create your printable or checklist on Canva – or all three! You can also offer your reader magnets on your social media platforms to help grow your email subscriber list there as well. **It is now time to create your magnet(s).**

**2. Set up your email platform.** If you don't already have an email list, go ahead and get yourself started with the free plan for now. Personally, I've used MailerLite for years. It's simple and fairly easy to use, and reasonably priced for what you get. As you're reviewing your options for email platforms, make sure you choose one that offers you an ability to set up landing pages and autoresponders.

**3. Create a book subscriber list on your email platform**, so you know where the emails are coming from. (Your book!) You may be tempted to just dump everybody one general email list to make things easier on yourself as you are starting out, but I'd urge you to reconsider. First, creating unique lists for each platform (ie your book versus your Instagram) where your reader encounters your reader magnet lets you know where your content is resonating with your clients and readers. Second, tagging or differentiating your list further, by each specific magnet, allows you to see some good hard data on all kinds of useful metrics – especially, which one of your magnets is the most exciting to your audience, and even better, it will enable you to find out who your superfans are – because they'll download everything you offer.

**4. Create a landing page and an email autoresponder** to add your readers to the mailing list you set up and deliver your reader magnet to them automatically. This probably sounds more complicated than it is – it should take you all of about 5 minutes to set up. Within your email platform, you should have the option to easily create a landing page.

Once your reader clicks on the landing page link, they'll be directed to a web form, where they'll enter their first name and email address. This will automatically trigger any email autoresponder you've set up.

Once your landing page is set up, create an email that will auto-send your email magnet to your subscriber immediately. If your email platform does not give you the option to host a download, you can use a third-party platform like Bookfunnel which is an inexpensive and reliable platform to host your reader magnets on. (They'll even integrate directly with your email platform and add those subscribers to the list you specify automatically!)

If you're not quite ready to set up your email platform quite yet, you can just use Bookfunnel to host your magnet, and they'll collect all the email addresses for you until you're ready to get yourself set up with a platform like MailerLite or MailChimp.

**5. Include the link (or a QR code of your link) at least once** somewhere in the text of your book, especially an Action Plan chapter, in addition to including it at the very beginning of your Resources chapter. You'll definitely want to include the link for your email magnet in multiple places – including the text of a relevant chapter of your book, as well as at the beginning of your Resources chapter.

Remember to consider both print and ebook readers as you include your links. Why? Ebook readers can actually generally click on a live link within the text of the book itself, whereas print readers can't.

- This is why you'll want to consider using short links in your print books, and including live links (as well as the URL) in the Resources section, like this: **Bestselling Author Writing Coach YouTube channel:** www.author.coach

- A QR code for your reader magnet landing page can also make life easier for your print book readers and I absolutely love Kindlepreneur's free QR code maker for authors! (Link in the Resources chapter.) It's free, super-easy to use, and you can customize the color and central image.

## WRITE NOW. Bestseller Book Building Blocks:

- **Create at least one reader magnet right now to include in your book.**

- **Set up an email platform** if you haven't already. If you don't already have an email list, go ahead and get yourself started with the free plan for MailerLite or MailChimp.

- **Create a subscriber list on your email platform**, so you know where the emails are coming from. (Your book!)

- **Create a landing page and an email autoresponder** to add your reader to the mailing list you set up and deliver the reader magnet automatically.

- **Include the link** (and/or a QR code of your link) **at least once** somewhere in the text of your book, especially an Action Plan chapter, in addition to including it at the very beginning of your Resources chapter.

# Chapter 12

# Create Your Workbook

Does your reader need a workbook to help them get the most out of your book?

Hmmm... Want to engage your readers in a more interactive and impactful way, and make some extra money without much effort?

Consider creating a workbook to accompany your self-help book. Workbooks are an invaluable resource that can enhance your reader's experience and provide numerous benefits to both of you.

Workbooks are extremely helpful for readers, helping them separate the strategy to accomplish their goals from the tactics they'll need to do so.

If you're on the fence, or thinking, *I don't want to worry about that now, Lisa,* just hear me out.

## Workbooks give you two books for the effort of one.

A workbook essentially takes all your steps and homework throughout your book and puts it into a convenient format that the reader can use to *write their own thoughts and notes*, specific to the problem they're trying to solve – or follow along with their end-of-chapter homework assignments, all in one place.

A workbook generally has the same cover as the original book, with the word WORKBOOK slapped up there somewhere. That's right, two books for the price of one cover, Woohoo!

Like this:

Using a nearly identical cover will help readers realize that the books go together, and that the workbook is a companion to help them get the most out of your primary book.

Not every one of your readers will buy your workbook, but many will.

But... Bonus! Some readers will even buy *multiple* copies of your workbook, for each time they go through the process. For example, many of my book coaching clients use a new workbook for each new book idea, so they can start fresh each time they start a new project.

## Workbooks are easy to create using content from your book

At this point, you've already done the heavy lifting by writing your self-help book. Now, think of your workbook as an extension of that content. You can repurpose key concepts, exercises, and strategies from your book to form the basis of your workbook.

You've also already structured your self-help book in a way that makes it easy for your reader to learn what you're trying to teach them, with your key takeaways and/or homework at the end of each chapter. Good news! All you need to do is take those key takeaways and homework assignments and put them all in one place, along with space for your reader to write their own answers, thoughts, and more.

Creating a workbook for your self-help book is a fairly straightforward and rewarding process, because it's pretty easy to repurpose the content you've already developed.

Let's break it down into manageable steps:

1. **Collect all your end-of-chapter homework exercises** into a single document to make organizing your information easier.

2. **Use Canva or another design platform to design your pages.** Don't be afraid to use templates and customize them to fit your book, Canva has free customizable templates to quickly create your own workbook pages.

3. **Design with accessibility in mind:** Keep the layout and design of your workbook clean, intuitive, and visually appealing. Break up text with headings, bullet points, numbered lists, pull quotes, and visuals to make it easy for your readers to navigate and engage with your material.

4. **Write a short introduction** at the beginning of your workbook that references your expertise and states the goal the reader is trying to accomplish. TIP: You can

just abbreviate chapters 1 and 2 of your self-help book to use in your workbook!

5. **Structure your workbook** by mirroring the chapters in the book so that readers can easily find the homework for each chapter quickly. (Meaning chapter 7 in your book, and chapter 7 in your workbook should both cover the same topic.)

6. **Add in blank or lined pages:** with enough space so that your readers have plenty of space to complete their assignments and reflect on what you've taught them.

7. **Add some pull quotes** from your book to create visual interest in your workbook and keep your reader motivated.

8. **Consider adding in a few additional prompts** or exercises you did not include in the book if you have some that may be helpful to your reader as they work towards accomplishing their goal.

9. **Simplify and adapt:** Remember, your workbook doesn't need to be lengthy or complex. Keep the exercises simple, actionable, and easy to understand. Adapt the exercises from your book to fit the workbook format, focusing on clarity and practicality.

10. **Graphically highlight links or QR codes** for all of

your reader magnets in the chapters where you first introduced them in the book.

11. **Mention your book regularly.** Remind your workbook readers that they can get the full explanation for each chapter by referring back to your original book.

12. **Include an abridged version** of The Future and Beyond as well as the Give Your Contact Info sections from the book.

13. **Include the exact same Resources section from your self-help book**, including all of your reader magnets.

You want to create a workbook that complements and enhances the impact of your self-help book, making it even more valuable to your readers on their journey of personal growth and transformation.

## How many pages does a workbook need to be?

You can publish a paperback workbook via Amazon KDP with as few as 24 pages, and via Ingram Spark with as few as 18. (I'd go ahead and do at least 24 pages across the board – you can always add in a few extra pages for introspection and reflection if you're a few short.)

## What if I don't have any design skills?

Don't sweat it. In addition to the free resources available on Canva (search "workbook pages") you can get some fantastic, professionally-designed, practically-done-for-you customizable workbook templates on Etsy, usually for less than $10.

What's great about Etsy templates (aside from the fact that they're beautiful, easy to use, and generally inexpensive) is that you can often find workbook templates in your book's specific niche. Search Etsy for "workbook template", "Canva workbook template", or "YOUR NICHE workbook template" –ie, "manifestation workbook template" or "diet workbook template" or "wellness workbook template".

## Why self-help readers love workbooks

Here are a few reasons why self-help readers love workbooks:

**1. Actionable Exercises:** Self-help readers are always looking for practical tools and exercises they can use to improve their lives or solve their problems. A workbook allows readers to easily and directly apply the principles, strategies, and techniques discussed in your book to their own lives, projects, or businesses, making your content more tangible and actionable.

**2. Personal Reflection**: Self-help is all about personal growth, introspection, and change. Workbooks offer space for your readers to reflect on their thoughts, feelings, and experiences, allowing them to gain deeper insights into themselves and their behaviors. This type of guided introspection can lead to profound personal transformation.

**3. Goal Setting and Tracking**: Your workbook can include sections for readers to set goals and track their progress. Self-help readers tend to be goal-oriented individuals who are motivated by their progress and growth. By providing a structured framework for goal setting and tracking based on the lessons you teach in your book, your workbook can help your readers to stay accountable and motivated on their journey toward achieving their goals.

**4. Customization**: Every person is unique, and self-help readers appreciate content that they can tailor to their own specific circumstances and needs. Workbooks offer a high level of customization (for both you and the reader), allowing readers to adapt your exercises and activities to meet their own goals and challenges.

**5. Community and Support**: Many self-help readers are part of various online communities, such as Facebook groups or Discord, where they can connect with others who are on a similar quest. If you offer such a group to your clients or readers, workbooks can help promote your community building efforts by providing opportunities for your readers to share their experiences, insights, and challenges with each other. This sense of connection and support can be incredibly motivating and empowering.

**6. Measurable Results**: Self-help readers are looking for concrete results and outcomes – they're reading your book to change their life! Workbooks offer a way for your readers to track their progress and see measurable results towards their goals as they work through your book over time, and provide a tangible framework for measuring success.

**7. You'll be ahead of the game if you decide to turn your self-help book into a class.** There's no need to reinvent the wheel – you can use most or all of your workbook pages as downloadable materials for your course. I love it when the content you've worked so hard to create does double duty, don't you?

Not sure you want to create a second book for sale? You can always create a downloadable workbook as a reader magnet.

Don't overlook the potential of workbooks to elevate your content and connect with your readers on a deeper level.

## WRITE NOW. Bestseller Book Building Blocks:

- **Use a free workbook template** on Canva to customize and create your own workbook for your self-help book, or buy a customizable template on Etsy.

- **Create your own workbook** either as a separate book for sale, or as a free reader magnet.

# Chapter 13

# Decide whether to publish yourself or traditionally

Traditional publishing? Self-publishing? Which is the better option for you?

I'm fortunate to have experienced both traditional publishing (Penguin, Random House UK, St. Martin's Press, Sourcebooks) as an author, and as Director for a mid-sized traditional publisher, as well as independently (indie) publishing myself – so my views on the matter are based on years of experience. (Fun fact: authors who publish both traditionally and independently are called "hybrid" authors.)

Both strategies have their pros and cons, and what you're hoping to get out of the process will dictate whether the indie or traditional publishing route is best for you.

## Traditional publishing

Let's break down the pros and cons of traditional publishing, shall we?

Traditional publishing is a method of publication where a publisher will offer you money (an advance) for the rights to publish your book. In exchange, they will cover the costs of editing, cover design, distribution, and provide some (but not much) marketing support, and take a good-sized chunk of the money you earn.

**Pros:**

- **Money up front.** You'll get paid an advance before the book ever goes on sale. The average advance for a debut author, according to Reedsy, is $5,000 - $10,000.

- **No upfront costs.** Your publisher, not you, will be paying for the editing, cover design, interior design, ISBN number, and most of the other upfront costs necessary to publish your book.

- **Status.** There's still a (small) stigma attached to indie publishing within the industry, although most consumers don't know or care who publishes the books they read. For many authors, a traditional publishing deal is the dream and the ultimate validation.

- **Distribution advantage.** If you're with a "Big 5" publisher – you're more likely to get your book carried in-store by a national chain like Barnes & Noble. (Although this is not guaranteed, and seems to be less and less certain.) They also have established distribution channels and relationships that *can*, but are not guaranteed to, help you reach a wider audience via libraries and booksellers.

**Cons:**

- **Literary agent.** You'll most likely need a literary agent to get a traditional publishing deal (not always, but usually) which will probably take you some time to find. Your agent will take a 15% cut of your earnings on domestic sales, and 20% (or more) if they're working with a co-agent to sell your foreign rights. Agents can be awesome and incredibly helpful to your career, but you always want to consider the big picture.

- **Cover.** The good news? They'll pay the cover designer. The bad news? If you hate your cover, you're stuck with it.

- **Right of refusal.** If your publisher wants changes to your manuscript, you have the right to refuse, but they can cancel your contract.

- **You earn less. A lot less.** You'll earn in the neighborhood of 5 - 8% royalties for paperback (trade paper, the format most likely to be carried by booksellers generally earns 7.5%) and 15-20% royalties for hardcover sales, and 20- 25% royalties for ebook sales.

- **Marketing will be dismal.** Unless your publisher paid a rare ($100K +) advance, the publisher will do very little to market your books, leaving that responsibility to you. The days of book tours are pretty much over for all but the top 1% of authors unless you make them happen yourself.

- **12-18 months from deal to publication.** On average, it takes about 16 months from deal to publication, not including the time it takes you to find an agent, and the time it takes the agent to sell your book to a publisher.

- **12 to 18-month delay on royalties.** There's no getting around it, publishing is a quill and ink business. On average, from the day a book is sold to a reader, it can take 12 to 18 months for you to see the money in your bank account. First, you'll need to earn out your advance before you see any additional royalties, and only about 25% of traditionally published books "earn out." Then, your publisher will hold a portion of your royalties "against returns" because publishing still uses an antiquated business model (sort of like consignment) where booksellers can return books that haven't sold back to publishers months and months (and months and months) later. Publishers hold your money for an extended time to guard themselves against this.

- **Less flexibility.** If you want to try a different pricing structure, put your book on sale, release in every format at the same time, or change your description or metadata – you'll have to get your publisher to agree to it, and then actually do the work for you. The bad news? They're already overworked and underpaid, and most of the time, your in-house editor or publicist won't want to deal with it.

- **You'll need to write a book proposal.** This is basically a marketing plan for your book, that explains to publishers who you are, what your platform is, and what the competition will be for your book idea. I created a YouTube video on this topic a few years ago on my Bestselling Author Writing Coach channel, *How to Write a Self-Help Book Proposal That Sells,* which you can watch free here: https://youtu.be/6dFfWMQEqDw

- **It's tougher to get traditionally published.** There are multiple gatekeepers, and both agents and publishers are inundated with manuscripts. Your odds of getting a traditional publishing deal are just 1-2%, according to WordsRated

## Indie publishing (also known as self-publishing)

**Pros:**

- **You get to keep all the money.** This is probably the biggest plus when it comes to indie publishing. Instead of splitting your book income with your publisher and your literary agent, you get to keep it all to yourself. While indie publishing your books is by no means a guaranteed path to riches, in my unique book coaching practice, **all** of my 6- and 7-figure authors are either self-published or hybrid-published.

- **It's a lot more money.** Indie authors earn up to 70% royalties on ebooks across the major retailers (Amazon, Apple, Google Play, Barnes & Noble, if the book is priced in the $2.99 to $9.99 range, or 35% - 45% if not.) Royalties for print books are more fluid, depending on interior color, number of pages, and a variety of other factors controlled by you. Generally, though, you'll earn between 25% - 55% on hardcover and paperback. You can see what your royalty rate will be and adjust the pricing up or down to reach your royalty target. (Note: KDP has a <u>handy tool</u> for this.) Compare that to a traditional publishing deal, where you have no say on the price of the book, and you'd expect to earn 5 - 8% royalties for paperback, 15-20% royalties for hardcover, and 20- 25% royalties for ebooks.

- **Royalties every 30 Days.** While indie publishing will not give you an advance like traditional publishing will, once the royalties start rolling in, you'll get paid by retailers like Amazon every 30 days. (I believe it's 60 days from the time of publication to your first royalty payment, but after that, it's every month.

- **You can mostly distribute your books like the Big 5.** Thanks to Amazon, Barnes & Noble, Draft 2 Digital, and Ingram Spark, you can basically replicate the same distribution the Big 5 have – with very few exceptions. While you probably won't have a dedicated sales force like a traditional publisher, you can easily have your book distributed through all the major online retailers and available for sale to brick-and-mortar bookstores and libraries as well. One major advantage of traditional publishing has always been its distribution – but that's becoming obsolete.

- **More flexibility and control.** If you want to try a different pricing structure, put your book on sale, make it free for a few weeks, release in every format at the same time, change your description, categories, or metadata you can just...do it! This makes it far easier to take advantage of time-sensitive marketing opportunities such as BookBub. You can change covers for a series that isn't selling well, do multiple versions, and about a million other things, because you own and control the rights to your book.

- **Publish in 1-3 days.** You can have a pre-order link up across all the major retailers within 24-72 hours so people can buy the book before you even finish writing it. (NOTE: You won't get royalties until you publish, however.) And if you've got your manuscript, cover, and description ready to roll, you can be a published author within 24-72 hours. Now, just because you *can* publish in 3 days doesn't mean you *should* – sometimes it makes more sense marketing-wise to give yourself a longer window before publication.

- **Anyone can self-publish.** There is no gatekeeper. You can put your book for sale on every major retailer and a ton of the minor ones, all by yourself with just a few clicks.

- **You don't need a literary agent.** Unless you want

one. Many indie authors self-publish in the US and English-speaking markets, and work with a foreign rights agent to sell rights in other countries. The cut is generally 20-25%, but as far as I'm concerned, this is found money for work you've already done, that you wouldn't have otherwise. In other words, if a foreign rights agent gets me a translation deal for 10K on one of my books, and I have to pay a $2500 commission on money I wouldn't have otherwise gotten, I'll be smiling all the way to the bank. (Okay, who am I kidding – that foreign rights money would most likely be wired directly into my account, no trip to the bank necessary.)

- **You don't need to keep a garage full of books.** Unlike the old days of self-publishing, nearly all book formats are printed on demand by Amazon, Barnes & Noble, or Ingram. That means the retailer or distributor doesn't print your hardcover or paperback until a customer or bookstore orders it.

**Cons:**

- **You cover expenses for editing, cover design, etc.** You will be paying for the editing, cover design, manuscript formatting, ISBN number, and most of the other upfront costs necessary to publish your book. Depending on your skill set, available time, and other factors, this can run you hundreds to thousands of dollars. It's possible, but not necessarily recommended, to edit your book yourself (or barter and trade manuscripts with another author), design your cover on a free design platform such as Canva, and publish your book as an ebook for free.

- **Stigma, if you care.** There's still a small stigma attached to indie publishing within the industry – although it's always funny to me that the same folks who look down their noses at indie authors are falling all over themselves to mimic them when it comes to how they market their books. (Seriously.) The truth is, most readers don't care or know who publishes the books they read and love, unless there's a quality issue.

- **Quality control is all on you.** The good news? You have control over everything. The bad news? You have control over *everything*. If you're a good project manager, you'll be fine. If not, you may need some assistance or guidance.

- **Marketing is also on you.** The good news? This is pretty much true whether you traditionally- or indie-publish your books. The job of finding your audience is yours, and it's a lonely, never-ending one. For advice and strategy on getting publicity yourself as a self-help author, check out ***Become a Famous Self-Help Author***: *PR Secrets to get TONS of Book Reviews & Free Publicity*

So which option is a better fit for you and your self-help book? Here are a few things to consider:

1. I have a unique book coaching specialty with quite a few 6 and 7-figure authors. *Every single one* of them is either an indie or hybrid author.

2. If you have a speaking, training, or coaching business, you already have a great opportunity for group sales. (Just tack on the cost for a thousand copies for attendees to your next speaking contract, or send out some email blasts to your subscriber base.) Do you really want to split that with your publisher? Yeah, me either.

3. If you don't feel comfortable with technology or DIY projects, you may want to consider traditional publishing. Or, you may choose to go ahead with self-publishing, and hire someone to do all the stuff a traditional publisher would typically do for you.

**If you need help**, that's exactly what I do every single day for a living – and I absolutely love it. Don't hesitate to book a call to chat with me or my awesome team. Please visit https://tidycal.com/lisadaily/book-coaching-intro to chat.

I offer multiple services and packages to help you accomplish each and every step listed in this book.

# Chapter 14

# The Parking Lot (aka, FAQ)

I want to start this chapter by saying I never, ever, have actually named a chapter title "The Parking Lot" until now, but I've referred to it by that name so frequently throughout this book that I wanted to make sure you understood exactly how the parking lot is used when you're writing your book, and see a real-life example in this book.

Below are some of the most commonly asked questions from my Bestseller Academy students and book coaching clients:

## What's the biggest mistake authors make when writing a self-help book?

The biggest mistake authors make is failing to keep the reader's needs in mind at all times, versus focusing on the author's needs.

Bear in mind, both your needs as an author (building an email list, selling coaching packages, etc) and the reader's needs (getting over whatever has them stuck and helping them accomplish their goal) do not need to be mutually exclusive.

**In fact, it works best when you can make those needs work together.**

Focus on your reader, write in second person, and provide tools that will help them accomplish their goal as quickly and easily as possible. Do that and the rest will take care of itself.

## What's the BIGGEST MISTAKE most first-time authors make (the one that makes you look like a JERK)?

One of the biggest mistakes I see first-time authors make is failing to keep their reader front of mind when writing their self-help book. What does this look like? If you've focused on yourself instead of your reader, your book will be all about you, what you think, what you're trying to do with your book to build your business, etc.

**A good self-help book keeps the reader and solving their pain points as the focus at all times.** Your experiences are valuable because they help the reader – **but make no mistake, your book must be all about *them*, and how you can help them to accomplish their goals.**

## Can anybody write a self-help book?

Absolutely! The beauty of self-help lies in its inclusivity. Anyone with a passion for helping others, a unique perspective, and a willingness to share their insights can embark on the exhilarating journey of writing a self-help book. Whether you're an expert in your field or a passionate novice, the world needs your voice, your experiences, and your unique approach to guide others on their paths of self-discovery.

## What are the secret strategies for making my book more appealing to the media and readers?

Good news, the strategy to do this is baked right into the Bestseller Academy Blueprint: It's your catchy plan name, clear action plan for the reader, and reader magnet freebies. Done and done!

## Do you have to be qualified to write a self-help book?

While formal qualifications definitely add credibility, they are not a strict prerequisite for writing a self-help book. What matters most is your passion, your insights, and your ability to communicate effectively. Your unique experiences and perspective can resonate with readers on a personal level, making your book more impactful than a string of letters after your name.

## How do you upsell your readers your courses and coaching in your book without being salesy?

One of the key ways to do this is with your reader magnets – by creating and nurturing a relationship with your reader via useful bonuses and regular email contact.

The second is in offering your services to **bridge the gap** between what your clients can and are willing to do for themselves and your wealth of expertise and experience.

For example, if you buy this book, download the free goodies, and follow the steps, you can ABSOLUTELY write a self-self book on your own. I've done everything I can to remove all the barriers to your success, and show you exactly what you need to do.

**But, for some of my readers who either want to get their books done faster, skip the learning curve, avoid costly mistakes, or just enjoy collaborating with a coach,** I also offer the Bestseller Academy Write a Self Help Book in 30 Days course, and one-on-one coaching.

The way to upsell your coaching, courses, and products without feeling like a used car salesman may seem counterintuitive: provide every possible thing you can so that your readers can accomplish their goal **with just the book** – but let them know that if they want or need a more hands-on approach, that you offer services or products to help.

## How much do self-help books make?

The answer varies wildly from almost nothing to millions of dollars. The income potential for self-help books varies significantly. Successful self-help authors can generate substantial income through book sales, speaking engagements, courses, coaching, memberships, mastermind groups, and other related opportunities. However, financial success is never guaranteed, and your success with writing a self-help book is largely dependent on how you use and market the book to build your business.

Personally, I earn six figures from my books and book-related income.

One major key to success is writing your book with the intention of using it to build your business, and keeping your eyes open for opportunities along the way to do just that.

## How many words should a self-help book be?

Your self-help book should be long enough to fully address the issue you're trying to solve for the reader, and should generally meet reader expectations for the genre, meaning somewhere in the sweet spot of 20,000-60,000 words.

That said, it's better to run a little shorter or longer than that guideline, rather than bloating your word count just to hit a number, or leaving out crucial elements to save words. What's most important is to write a good book that addresses your reader's needs.

## What classifies a book as self-help?

A book is classified as self-help if its primary purpose is to offer guidance, advice, or insights to help readers improve their lives. Self-help books (also called self-improvement) cover a broad spectrum of topics, including personal development, relationships, mental health, earning money, and other practical skills. The common thread is the intent to empower and inspire positive change in your reader.

## I already tried to write a self-help book on my own, but got stuck. How can I get unstuck and salvage what I wrote?

Great question, and frankly, it's where many of my book-coaching clients start out. The answer is to start from the beginning with the Creative Work Plan, and follow the plan from there. Most of my book coaching clients who have started and gotten stuck initially sort of launched into their books with what will eventually become the Action Plan chapters, without any lead-up or focus on the reader's pain points. In this case, you'll want to start at the beginning with the Creative Work Plan, write your first two chapters according to the Bestseller Academy Blueprint, and then see where you are as far as what you've already written. You may just want to stick your entire early version in the Parking Lot, and just cut and paste relevant sections as you work your way through the Blueprint.

## What should I do if I need help?

> If you need help, that's exactly what I do every single day for a living – I'm here for you! Feel free to book a call to chat with me or my awesome team to get your questions answered. Please visit https://tidycal.com/lisadaily/book-coaching-intro to chat.
>
> I offer multiple services and packages to help you accomplish each and every step listed in this book.

## Is there a course for writing a self-help book?

Yes! I'm so glad you asked. The Bestseller Academy course is one of the few classes available that teach you to write a self-help book step by step, using the strategy in this book.

The course features a deeper dive into the materials you've learned in this book, with additional videos and downloadable materials to get your self-help book done FAST. Plus, we'll be doing some live calls to help you tackle the biggest challenges of writing a self-help book, not to mention access to an incredible online community.

**Find out more and register at BestsellerAcademy.courses and save $50 using the code BESTSELLER50.**

## Have a question for me?

Do you have a question that isn't addressed here or elsewhere in the book? Drop me a line at heylisa@lisadailybooks.com and I'll do my best to answer it.

## You've got this.

I'm super proud of you for making it this far! Yay!!!!! You did it!!!

Believe me, nobody understands what a major undertaking it can be to write a self-help book like I do. And look how much progress you've made!

Your ideas, experiences, and wisdom can now help others to accomplish their goals, solve a problem, or just lead happier and more successful lives. Do you know what a big deal that is? It's huge!

I'd really love to hear about your experience writing your book, and any challenges you've faced along the way. (Or anything you loved or think I might have missed!)

I'm super excited to hear more about your awesome book and all the cool things you'll be doing with it!

**Let's stay in touch:**

Email: heylisa@lisadailybooks.com

LisaDailyBooks.com

Instagram: @authorbythesea

Bestseller Academy BestsellerAcademy.courses

Bestselling Author Writing Coach YouTube channel: www.author.coach

## CHAPTER 15

# Resources to Help You Write Your Self-Help Book & Build Your Business

**Free Tools & Goodies From Me to Get You Started**

**A**ll the goodies in one place! If you'd like ALL the awesome resources (with links!) for this book (including the free fillable Google doc of the Creative Work Plan and Bestseller Academy Blueprint, plus a bunch of freebies and bonuses), sent to your email, just use the QR code or click here.

## The Course

### The Bestseller Academy: Write a Self-Help Book in 30 Days.

*Open the camera app on your phone to click the QR code to get all the free goodies and bonuses to write your book quickly and easily.*

A hands-on, medium-pace course to guide you write your self-help book, step-by-step in an online class setting. Includes video lessons, printables to help your writing process go smoothly and easily, live Q&As with me, problem-focused Zoom calls to tackle your biggest challenges (like coming up with your title or your reader magnets), accountability, a private Facebook Group, and some truly epic bonuses. Let's get your book done this month!

GET $50 OFF YOUR **WRITE A SELF-HELP BOOK IN 30 DAYS COURSE** WHEN YOU USE THE CODE **BESTSELLER50**

BestsellerAcademy.courses

## More Books to Help You Succeed

***Write a Self-Help Book in 14 Days Workbook*** — This handy workbook keeps all your exercises and tools in one gorgeous place to help you stay organized as you're writing your self-help book.

***Become a Famous Self-Help Author*** — Everything you need to know to pitch the media as a self-help author, and become a known expert in your field.

***What 7-Figure Authors Do Differently*** — I've spent the last several years as a book coach for 6- and 7-figure authors, and what I've learned about how they run their author businesses will cause you to re-think everything you're doing. And you should...

## One-on-One Book Coaching

If you need help or you'd like to finish your book faster, that's exactly what I do – and it's one of my all-time favorite things in the Universe.

Don't hesitate to book a free "get to know you" call to chat with me or my awesome team. Please visit https://tidycal.com/lisadaily/book-coaching-intro to chat.

I offer multiple services and packages to help you accomplish each and every step listed in this book.

## Free Videos

Here are a few helpful videos from my Bestselling Author Writing Coach YouTube channel, www.Author.coach

*How to Structure Self-Help Books*: https://www.youtube.com/watch?v=DPws94zqWcA&t=3s&list=UULPe36_egPO62qjzjF-cNO44g

*How to Write a Bestselling Self-Help Book | 3 Things You Need to Know*: https://youtu.be/MzxpzZd57vg

*How to Write a Self-Help Book Proposal That Sells*: https://youtu.be/6dFfWMQEqDw

## A Few of the Books I Mentioned

*Write a Self-Help Book in 14 Days WORKBOOK* by Lisa Daily

*Become a Famous Self-Help Author: PR Secrets to Become a Recognized Expert and Get Tons of Free Publicity* by Lisa Daily

**What 7-Figure Authors Do Differently** by Lisa Daily

*Make Time: How to Focus on What Matters Every Day* by Jake Knapp and John Zeratsky.

*7-Figure Fiction* by T. Taylor

*Write to Riches* by Renee Rose

*The Bestselling Author Next Door* by Skye Warren

*Adventures with the Universe* by Lee Savino

*Manifest Your HEA* by Heather Hildenbrand

*Rule Your Authordom* by Kel Carpenter

*Books to TV & Film* by Maggie Marr

## Other Helpful Stuff

MailerLite or MailChimp Email marketing platform. (Free; *My link saves you $20 on paid plan once you have enough subscribers you're ready to upgrade.)

Bookfunnel.com Host your reader magnets and integrate with your email list

Publisher Rocket Find Amazon keywords, categories and more – one of my all-time favorite publishing tools, I've been using for more than a decade. https://authorlisadaily--rocket.thrivecart.com/publisher-rocket/ (*Affiliate ink)

Canva.com Free templates to build your workbook

Etsy.com Inexpensive ( usually for less than $10) customizable templates for your niche

Typeform.com SurveyMonkey.com Paperform.co, or Buzzfeed to create quizzes (Gryffindor Method)

Teachable Easily build a course from your book

Tool to estimate your print royalties for KDP: https://kdp.amazon.com/en_US/royalty-calculator

Kindlepreneur's free QR code maker for authors: https://kindlepreneur.com/qr-code-generator-for-authors/

## I want to hear about your book!

**I'm so proud of you for taking on this incredible project.** Your book has the power to transform your readers' lives, your status in your chosen profession, and even your business. This book of yours can change your readers' worlds and yours — and I couldn't be more proud and thrilled to be your guide along this journey.

**Let's stay in touch, I'm excited to hear how you're doing!**
Email: heylisa@lisadailybooks.com
LisaDailyBooks.com
Instagram: @authorbythesea
Bestseller Academy BestsellerAcademy.courses
My Bestselling Author Writing Coach YouTube channel: www.author.coach

Keep writing and let me know how you're doing!

xoxo,

Lisa

www.ingramcontent.com/pod-product-compliance
Lightning Source LLC
Chambersburg PA
CBHW070623030426
42337CB00020B/3895